SOCIOLOGICAL THEORY

—

A CONTEMPORARY VIEW

HOW TO READ, CRITICIZE AND DO THEORY

———

Neil J. Smelser

——

with a 2011 Foreword by Arlie Russell Hochschild

Classics of the Social Sciences Series

qp

Quid Pro Books

New Orleans, Louisiana

Sociological Theory — A Contemporary View
How to Read, Criticize and Do Theory

Originally published in 1971 by General Learning Press, New York, New York, under the title of *Sociological Theory: A Contemporary View.*

Published in the 2011 edition by Quid Pro Books. Available in print and multiple digital editions.

ISBN: 1610270525
ISBN-13: 9781610270526

Quid Pro, LLC
5860 Citrus Blvd., Suite D-101
New Orleans, Louisiana 70123
www.quidprobooks.com

Cover photograph copyright © 2009 by Paul Szustka, used by permission. Author photograph copyright © 2009 by Al Weber, used by permission.

ꝗP

Publisher's Cataloging-in-Publication

Smelser, Neil J.

Sociological theory — a contemporary view: how to read, criticize and do theory / Neil J. Smelser.

p. cm.

Includes bibliographical references and index of sections.

Includes 2011 Preface and Foreword.

Series: *Classics of the Social Sciences.*

ISBN: 1610270525 (pbk., 2011)
ISBN-13: 9781610270526 (pbk., 2011)
ISBN: 1610270509 (Kindle)
ISBN: 1610270517 (ePub)

1. Sociology. 2. Sociology—Theory. 3. Sociology—History. 4. Sociologists—Biography. I. Title. II. Series.

HM 24 S5321 2011   301'.02—dc22

TABLE OF CONTENTS

A more detailed listing of sections and subsections is found at the back, as the Index of Sections. Both the Index and this Table of Contents are keyed to the original page numbers of the previous edition, as embedded in the text using {brackets}, and as shown below within brackets. This allows continuity of referencing and citation. The Table of Contents also shows the modern pagination of the book, unbracketed.

Note from the Series Editor

Most theorists pontificate without either much self-awareness or scrutiny from others. They and their often-passive audience often lack the tools to make that evaluation. They do not seem to mind, however, and so their work causes little in the way of impact on the surface of the Earth. There is a story that one professor was speaking at an academic conference, and afterwards a young admirer commented to him, "I found that to be very useful." The professor was mortified: "You didn't like it?"

Throughout the years, Neil Smelser has not fit that stereotype. His own work (some of which, fortunately, will be republished in this Series) has been up for the challenge over many generations of scholars and students. And he does not seem to mind that it has actually been, and continues to be, incredibly useful.

This monograph is particularly useful to the big thinkers and even the curious tinkerers who want to take apart social theory and see what makes it tick. Certainly they will be given the tools to read and examine it critically—with the relief of having some thoughtful standards by which to review and judge theory in the social sciences. They may even learn to create it themselves, and in the process do it with a useful measuring rod at hand. It should be read by those who want to see theory from the inside.

And so it is presented to the modern reader with an added subtitle— *How to Read, Criticize and Do Theory*—because that is what this book offers its consumers. Dr. Smelser was gracious to let me add that tagline, and I apologize to him and the reader if it sounds like modern puffery in the vein of how-to home repair books and DIY renovation websites. But it is only puffery if it does not deliver the goods. I am confident that this book does. Although it originated in a challenging undergraduate course at Berkeley about the hows and how-nots of sociological theory, it really does have current application in a variety of intellectual enterprises well deserving of the new subtitle.

The irony is that the original subtitle—*A Contemporary View*—still applies and was consciously retained. Even though this book was produced four decades ago, it retains a modern relevance, and indeed a timelessness, in two important ways. First, the theorists that Neil Smelser picked as examples are simply foundational and exemplary for any current understanding of sociological theory. It is not as if Durkheim and Marx, for example, can be ignored in digging into the theorizing we have inherited. Nor will his other applications seem outdated to students of today. Second, the fundamental criteria for systematically analyzing and criticizing theory have not changed. If whatever buzzes around journals, SSRN, and the internet today is to have any lasting value, it will have to pass muster under the tools of scrutiny so clearly described here.

As a model of systematic and clear thinking about theory, its value remains. In relatively few pages, and with accessible examples and core information, the author extracts the essence of very complex and abstract theoretical materials. All for the purpose of making them understandable to students and other readers in many fields who are first approaching the world of theoretical thinking. In the process, and in a surprising way given its accessible brevity, this book covers a lot of ground and is not limited to the U.S. canon. It thus has a reach and scope quite relevant, today and everywhere.

With no more puffery than that, and with every confidence that it continues to accomplish the important yet daunting task for which it was originally created, I am proud to bring this work back to a new generation of burgeoning theoretical critics or critical theorists.

Steven Alan Childress
Conrad Meyer III Professor of Law
Tulane University

FOREWORD

This is an important and timely book. In an era that calls out for insightful social theory, this book extends a welcome mat. It invites us not only to explore the ideas of great thinkers, but to apply to these an appraising eye that is both discerning and appreciative. So in this book, Neil Smelser does not simply describe theories or pick out biases in them. Instead, he offers us a template—itself a work of art—to hold up to any system of thought. Lucidly, appreciatively, he points out what we see when we compare what to look for with what a theorist gives us to see.

The book focuses on works from Émile Durkheim, Talcott Parsons, Karl Marx and Robert Michels. For each theory, he poses a series of probing questions. What is a theorist trying to understand? What are the basic concepts? How do these concepts logically relate to one another? (Is the theory coherent?) And how do we identify these concepts empirically? (How do we operationalize them?) Given a certain logical arrangement of concepts, what propositions can we derive from them? How can we test these propositions to see whether they are true or false? (Is the theory falsifiable?) And what can we conclude?

This book originated as an undergraduate course at the University of California, Berkeley. (As a graduate student auditor, I sat close up front, madly scribbling notes.) Emerging from a year in the British Museum where he had completed a dissertation on the British Industrial revolution, Neil Smelser, a former Rhodes Scholar who had studied philosophy, politics and economics at Oxford, his Harvard PhD newly in hand, arrived in 1958 at Berkeley to teach this course at the age of 28. The course, Sociology 109, began with 50 undergraduates and one teaching assistant. But over time, it became known as a tough, bracing, must-take course. Seven years later, enrollment had ballooned to 350 students, and teaching assistants to six. Students were assigned four essays, one on each theorist, and grades were based on the three best and a final exam. The T.A.s were given extra instruction on clear exposition, and Smelser made a point to himself visit each discussion session.

Though the class called for serious concentration, it also had its light moments. Caught one day without a babysitter, the desperate young Smelser brought his six-year-old son and four-year-old year old daughter to class. As they sat down, Smelser drew a chalk picture of a small cat on the blackboard. Students might have wondered which theorist the professor meant the cat to represent. Was it Marx? (Too quiescent.) Was it Parsons? (Too marginal.) Or was Smelser's cat like Flaubert's parrot, a quietly inspiring muse? Smelser explained, of course, that his daughter had requested him to draw the cat, and returned to his lecture. Sometime later an enormous dog lumbered down the main aisle on its way, so it seemed, to Smelser's cat. "I'm trying to increase the enrollment of auditors," Smelser quipped.

Since the days of Sociology 109, Smelser has gone on to a stunningly creative, wide-ranging and productive career that shows—through his very creativity—that holding to high standards of theory building needn't stop one from giving it a real go. Smelser's own first book, co-written when he was 25 with Talcott Parsons, was on society and economy. His second book explores a theory of structural differentiation, separating workplace from home, and family role from work ones, during the British industrial revolution. Another applies a "value-added" approach to understanding collective behavior—riots, crazes, social movements of various sorts. He extends this approach in his important, recent *Faces of Terrorism: Social and Psychological Dimensions* (2007). In yet another book, he opens a wondrous conceptual tool kit of psychoanalysis, and there offers up an idea I've used in my own work. Freud conceptualized mechanisms of defense as that which we direct against the threat of our inner instinctual urges. We can direct mechanisms of defense, Smelser further argues, toward our outer social environment as well. In a recent book, *The Odyssey Experience: Physical, Social, Psychological and Spiritual Journeys* (2009), Smelser draws on ancient myth, travel legends, anthropological ethnography and other sources to propose telltale signs of the "odyssey" experience.[*]

---

[*] *Economy and Society: A Study in the Integration of Economic and Social Theory* (1964), by Talcott Parsons and Neil Smelser, London: Routledge, & Kegan Paul; *Social Change in the Industrial Revolution: An Application of Theory to the British Cotton Industry* (2006) London: Routledge; *Theory of Collective Behavior* (1962) New York: Free Press; *The Faces of Terrorism: Social and Psychological Dimensions* (2007) Princeton: Princeton University Press; *America Becoming: Racial Trends and Their Consequences*, Vol. 2 (2001), by Faith Mitchell, Neil Smelser, William J. Wilson (eds.), National Research Council; *The Odyssey Experience:*

Sociological Theory – A Contemporary View is timeless, but also especially timely. For today, sociology finds itself increasing squeezed between two expanding neighboring paradigms—an economic paradigm to one side, and a biological paradigm to the other. In 1904, the early American Sociological Society broke away from the American Economic Society in an effort to develop a richer, less reductive perspective on society. Still, the economic paradigm is being applied to all manner of non-market life—small group behavior, marriage, divorce, the practice of adoption, for example. Implied in the paradigm—as Smelser has observed—is a reductive model of self. Instead of a complex, reflective self capable of ambivalence,[†] many economistically-minded theorists give us the interest-maximizing self as bargaining unit in a context of shifting supply and demand for desired goods.

From the other side biological determinists, and in particular geneticists, offer an image of the individual as a receptacle of powerful genes. A number have offered purely genetic explanations for such things as racial differences in scholastic achievement, alcohol consumption, gender roles and criminal behavior. Meanwhile bearing, perhaps, the mark of post-modernism, sociology has seemed to turn inward and, to some degree, lose interest and faith in "grand theory." This book is an invitation back; let's dare to build big theories, it tacitly says, and do it well.

Smelser explores four thinkers here, but he invites us to the world of sociological theory—Alexis deTocqueville, Sigmund Freud, Georg Simmel, Alfred Schutz, Karl Mannheim, Thorsten Veblen, Simon de Beauvoir, and many more. Indeed, this book prepares the reader for a great intellectual odyssey.

Arlie Russell Hochschild
Professor of Sociology
University of California, Berkeley
2011

Physical, Social, Psychological, and Spiritual Journeys (2009) Berkeley: University of California Press; *The Handbook of Economic Sociology* (2005) Princeton: Princeton University Press.

[†] *See, generally*, Neil J. Smelser, "The Rational and the Ambivalent in the Social Sciences," *American Sociological Review*, Vol. 63, No. 1, February, 1998, pp. 1-16.

PREFACE

IT is a great pleasure to witness the reappearance of my book, *Sociological Theory*, written as an accumulation of ideas that I had developed, honed, responded to criticisms by both sophisticated and naïve students, and re-worked through seven years (1958-1965) of teaching an undergraduate course by that name at Berkeley. I will confess (forty years later, now) that I have always regarded it as one of my strongest and most gratifying intellectual efforts—if not the most widely read. I agree with my colleagues that, in dealing with the "timeless" topic of the methodology of theoretical thinking, it continues and will continue to be timely for scholars and students alike. I would like to express my heartiest thanks to Alan Childress and Arlie Hochschild for organizing and overseeing the resurrection of this work.

I take advantage of this moment of republication to add a historical footnote about the book's development. In the winter of 1957, the sociology department of University of California, Berkeley and I were eyeing one another sympathetically about the prospect my joining its faculty as an Assistant Professor. When they offered me the job in November of that year, they specified only one mandatory teaching assignment: I was to offer the required upper-division theory course in systematic theory. The course was a new one, imposed on majors as one aspect, I suppose, of that department's bid for intellectual rigor and leadership in sociology in those postwar years. In asking me to teach this course, some of my Berkeley colleagues-to-be almost apologized to me for demanding some kind of servitude on my part. They could have not been more mistaken. I was fully committed to the theoretical enterprise in sociology, and, mainly as a student of and collaborator with Talcott Parsons at Harvard, I had been fully steeped in theory.

There was one other happy circumstance in this new assignment. I had completed my doctoral dissertation in December 1957, and had the following spring and summer entirely free. I did revise and shorten the dissertation for publication by the University of Chicago Press (*Social Change in the Industrial Revolution*, 1959), but I decided to devote the remainder of my time to preparing "my" new course. I selected the books after surveying many possibilities; read every one of them multiple times; hammered out the set of theoretical criteria I was going to employ; and wrote, re-wrote, and clarified the lectures. I have never work so hard or so thoroughly on a single course in my life. By the time I arrived in Berkeley in September of 1958, every lecture was ready. Since I had had virtually no teaching experience at that time (my graduate fellowship at Harvard prohibited teaching, even as a Teaching Fellow), I am certain that this luxury of full preparation in advance contributed to the value of the course for those who subsequently took it.

Neil J. Smelser
University Professor Emeritus of Sociology
University of California, Berkeley

Berkeley, California
February, 2011

SOCIOLOGICAL THEORY

—

A CONTEMPORARY VIEW

Neil J. Smelser

qp

Introduction

THE study of sociological theory is commonly divided into two types of academic courses: "History of Sociological Thought" and "Systematic Sociological Theory." In the former we examine critically the ideas of the great historical schools—utilitarianism, Marxism, idealism, sociological positivism, and so on—as espoused by their most articulate representatives; we ask how these schools of thought influenced one another and thereby produced a complicated mosaic of intellectual history; and we often ask how these intellectual positions affect the ways we think and work in sociology today. In courses in systematic theory, we deal more with modern writers; we explore the logic of theory construction and address questions of the philosophy of science; we try to understand what is meant by formal terms such as "models," "hypotheses," and "derivation"; and we study various verbal and mathematical modes of theorizing.

From an educational standpoint there may be a sound rationale for this kind of subdivision of sociological theory. From other standpoints, however, the subdivision into history of theory and systematic theory creates difficulties. First, it is difficult to draw any meaningful empirical line between the two aspects. Contemporary theory must be considered as a part of the history of theory, since history obviously runs right up to the present. Furthermore, I know of no point in time when "history of theory" turns into "systematic theory." From classical times to the present, many thinkers have been systematic; and many modern writers we call theorists can scarcely be called systematic in their approach. And some theorists—Marx, Weber, Durkheim, to name the most prominent ones—are at once influential figures in the history of social thought and very systematic in their theoretical conceptualization and empirical scholarship. {2}

I am going to try to cut through this troublesome distinction by adopting the following strategy. I shall assume that there is such an activity as *sociological theorizing* and that in pursuing this activity a thinker has to face a definite number of *issues* or *problems*. For example, in creating a theory, a thinker must be as explicit as possible in identifying what he is trying to explain; he must avoid logical contradictions and absurdities; and he must try to ascertain whether his theoretical ideas square with empirical reality. I assume that these issues are, in some respects, timeless; that it is possible to ask whether and how Adam Smith faced them, just as it is possible to ask whether and how any modern theorist faces them. By asking the same set of questions of all thinkers, we can thereby *compare* various theories with one another, even though they differ greatly. Furthermore, by asking how well thinkers face the issues that arise in theorizing, we are in a position to *evaluate* their theories as intellectual and scientific products.

My objective in this essay is to develop a series of questions that pinpoint the issues that arise in sociological theorizing. These questions constitute a set of tools that can be used to describe, criticize, and evaluate any sociological work. I shall then apply these questions more or less systematically to several very different sociological theorists—Émile Durkheim, Talcott Parsons, Karl Marx, and Robert Michels—in an effort to assess the strengths and weaknesses of the work of each. By this exercise I hope to sharpen students' abilities to evaluate critically, not only the work of these and other theorists, but their own theoretical thinking.

To evaluate the theoretical aspect of any scholar's thought is not to evaluate every aspect. There are other aspects as well—literary elegance, ideological potency, social utility, and so on—that can be assessed by applying canons other than those of theoretical adequacy. Furthermore, if and when we discover theoretical omissions or flaws in a body of thought, we are not necessarily scolding the scholar for not measuring up to his objectives. It may be that his intentions were not to create a sociological theory in the full sense we now conceive it. Nevertheless, it is still possible and profitable to inquire in what ways his work does and does not qualify as sociological theory.

I shall begin by making up a little theory of my own—a theory that attempts to explain the behavior of political parties during political campaigns. This theory has three virtues. First, it is simple, thereby permitting us to perceive the theoretical issues clearly. Second, it is hypothetical, thereby permitting us to imagine—rather than go out and discover—the facts that it attempts to explain. Third, since the theory is simple and hypothetical, it will be possible to build into it a weakness that can be readily identified. After presenting the theory, I shall outline the general issues that arise even in constructing such a simple theory.

The largest part of this essay will be devoted to analyzing some of the work of four major theorists in the European and American sociological tradition. I have chosen the following theoretical works:

Émile Durkheim's theory of suicide. It would be difficult not to include *Suicide* in our sample, since it has been so long and so widely regarded as a model of sociological research. In this book, written early in his career, Durkheim (1858-1917) took a fairly limited range of information—the suicide statistics available to him at the end of the nineteenth century—and erected a coherent and quite comprehensive theory of society to explain why some social groups are more prone to suicide than others. The principal thesis of the book is that social cohesion (and lack of cohesion) of different groups is the main cause of variations in suicide rates among these groups. Durkheim's theory is remarkably complete in that it faces directly, if not always satisfactorily, all the issues that arise in sociological theorizing.

Talcott Parsons' theory of deviant behavior. Parsons (born in 1902), one of the most widely known contemporary sociological theorists, has devoted his intellectual career principally to creating a general theory of social action, with particular attention to social systems. While Durkheim was one of the most important intellectual influences on Parsons, the latter's theory is more comprehensive than Durkheim's. He has extended it to the analysis of social stratification, the family, economic development and social evolution, behavior in small groups, development of personality, and to topics as specialized as psychosomatic disorders. From this array (and especially from *The Social System*) I shall infer some of the foundations of Parsons' social system theory and consider the application of this theory to the explanation of the genesis and control of various kinds of deviant behavior (for example, criminal activity).

Karl Marx's theory of capitalism. Marx (1818-1883) is best known, of course, as the creator of the foundations of an ideology that has spawned revolutionary movements and governments throughout the world in the past century. In his own lifetime, {3} Marx himself was certainly active as a revolutionary, but he devoted most of his energy to creating a comprehensive philosophy of history and theory of economic and social evolution. I shall focus on the first volume of *Das Kapital*—the most mature and comprehensive statement of Marx's theory of capitalism. As with the other theorists, I shall cover only selected aspects of Marx's work, concentrating mainly on the laws of development of capitalist society, exploitation, class conflict, and revolution.

Robert Michels' theory of political organization. Michels, a German-Italian sociologist (1876-1936), was exposed to and much influenced by Marxian and syndicalist thought early in his career. In his most important book, *Political Parties*, he undertook to analyze the internal structure of certain left-wing political groups in Western European countries around the turn of the century. His principal thesis was that these groups, despite their commitment to ideals of equality, fail to maintain these ideals in their own structures and instead develop rigid and permanent oligarchies. His formula of the "iron law of oligarchy" is an important sociological contribution. Since this formula strikes at the heart of both democratic and socialist theory, it has attracted widespread attention.

These several authors are diverse. The publication dates of their books span almost a century—Marx's *Capital* appeared first in 1867, Durkheim's *Suicide* in 1897, Michels' *Political Parties* in 1911, and Parsons' *The Social System* in 1951. Their works cover a large number of subfields of sociology—deviance, social movements, economic sociology, political sociology, social stratification, and social change. And several "schools of thought" are represented. Durkheim wrote *Suicide* at a time when he was committed to the school of "sociological positivism"; Parsons' work is most commonly assigned to the "structural-functionalist" tradition; Marx, it can be safely argued, falls in the "Marxist" tradition;[3] and while Michels' work obviously shows the influence of Marx, he is often grouped with Vilfredo Pareto, Gaetano Mosca, and others in the "Italian irrationalist" school of thought.

Despite this diversity, we are going to ask identical questions of each of these authors. This approach is justified, I feel, because each theorist selected some features of social life and attempted to develop an intellectual apparatus to explain them. Because they were engaged in the same general enterprise—however differently they went about

---

[3] Late in his life, however, apparently dismayed at some of the distortions of his work by some of his followers, Marx claimed "I am not a Marxist" in several letters.

it—a number of common intellectual issues arose for them. Let us now try to formulate these issues as simply as possible.

A Simple Model of Political Behavior

The notion of a model is based on a distinction commonly made in science: that between empirical phenomena (the "real" world) and the concepts we use to think about empirical phenomena (the "world of ideas").[4] A model, defined simply, is a construction of concepts, on the basis of which we make conditional predictions about what we expect to happen in the real world. A model may take the form of mathematical formulas, of words, or even pictures. An example of a model is the economist's theory of a business cycle. He arranges the economic concepts of savings, investment, consumption, and so forth, into a set of relations with one another in such a way that they permit predictions about the fluctuations of the economy. A model, then, consists of a network of statements organized so that we expect certain phenomena to occur empirically under specified conditions.

Two general criteria permit us to decide whether a model is a good one. (1) Its logical consistency, which concerns the conceptual structure of the model itself. Are the concepts defined clearly? Are their relations to one another spelled out explicitly? Are these relations logically consistent? (2) Its empirical validity, which concerns whether the facts of the real world conform to the hypothetical outcome predicted by the model. If they do not, a further question arises: can the model be made workable by modification, or must it be rejected?

Keeping these two different types of criteria in mind, I shall now construct a simple, illustrative model of political behavior and then indicate a possible test for the model.

---

[4] Even this apparently simple distinction opens a number of thorny philosophical problems. For two brief comments on the distinction, see "A Note on the Concept of Fact," pp. 41-42 in Parsons 1949 and pp. 58-59 in Smelser 1968.

The Model

Let us suppose that we have noticed on an impressionistic basis that the strategies and tactics of political leaders and party officials seem to vary at different {4} times in the electoral cycle. Big "scandals"—such as bribery in high government circles—seem to be "uncovered" as elections grow nearer but seldom in the immediate aftermath of elections. Personal attacks on political leaders also seem to vary in their timing and intensity. In constructing the following model we attempt to explain this kind of variability in behavior.

To simplify matters we shall limit our concern only to American politics and to presidential elections. Furthermore, we shall assume a two-party system, ignoring the possibilities of third parties and coalitions. We shall assume further that what determines the content and timing of different political tactics is *not* the ideological character of the party—that is, whether it is Democrat or Republican—but whether the party is in or out of office. We shall also assume that political tactics are initiated by the "out" party in the following sequence:

Phase 1. In the period immediately after the unsuccessful election, the outs will quietly patch their wounds and *search* for new modes of attack. This is a period of political quiescence.

Phase 2. The outs will attack the *policies* of the ins and claim that they are not governing the way the outs would if they were in power. For example, the outs accuse the ins of using the wrong monetary and fiscal policies to curb inflation.

Phase 3. The outs charge the ins with *administrative incompetence.* They claim the policies of the ins as their own and maintain they could implement them better. During the Eisenhower years, for example, Democrats claimed that the Republicans were merely following out the lines of New Deal policy, and doing a poor job of it.

Phase 4. The outs accuse the ins of *breaking the rules* of the political game. Scandals are uncovered, corruption is charged, cries of "foul play" are heard.

Phase 5. In the final phase before the next election, the outs *personally attack* the party leaders of the in party.

Again for the purposes of simplicity, we shall not list a corresponding set of phases for the in party but shall assume that their behavior is directed to defending themselves against the attacks of the outs.

This, then, is the model, or the set of expectations we have generated about political behavior of parties between elections. Our hypotheses describe the expected sequence of tactics to be pursued by the opposition party. This is the dependent variable, or what we want to explain. The independent or causal variable is the fact that the party is out of office, seeking to win the coming election.

Testing the Model

To see how well the model works in the empirical world, we have to decide on a number of indicators for the major variables in the model. The indicator for "political tactics" will be all official statements made by the headquarters of each party and by all members of Congress over a four-year period, as reported in *The New York Times*. We shall consider that a party is "in" when it controls the Presidency and "out" when it does not.

Once we have chosen these indicators for the major concepts, we must devise an empirical test that will either validate or reject the hypotheses generated by the model. First, we have to decide on the time duration of the five phases. For purposes of testing we shall assume that the sequence begins immediately after a presidential election, that each of the five phases is approximately equal in length, and that each phase lasts for about nine months. This may be an arbitrary assumption, but it locates the phases in time; it provides an empirical specification for the otherwise indeterminate concept of "phase." Second, we have to choose specific electoral campaigns for a test. In this connection we shall choose two periods—1936 to 1940 (Roosevelt's second term) and 1952 to 1956 (Eisenhower's first term). This is a small sample, but it does give us one period when each of the two major parties was in power.

The next step is to decide how to measure political tactics. For this we devise a set of code categories to classify the content of all political articles appearing in *The New York Times* in the relevant years (for example, "personal attacks," "attacks on policy"). Then we might have a panel of coders read and analyze the contents of the *Times;* if the coders agree among themselves, we shall assume we have a reliable index for political tactics.

Finally, we must compare the hypotheses with results obtained from actual data. For our model, we see that in hypothetical figure 1 the total incidence of all tactics initiated by the outs rises during the first two phases, then levels off. In figure 2, policy attacks predominate in the second phase, and in figures 3, 4, and 5 the other kinds of tactics cluster in time as predicted. Assume also that we apply a statistical test to these distributions and that these tests reveal that the clusterings are greater than could be expected by chance alone. We would, therefore, conclude that this model is adequate to account for the tactics of political parties in the United States in national elections, at least for the two periods tested. {5}

*Figures 1-5. Clustering of political tactics over time,
electoral periods 1936-40 and 1952-56.*

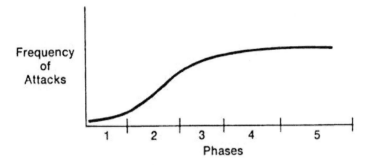

Figure 1. Total incidence of all types of tactics.

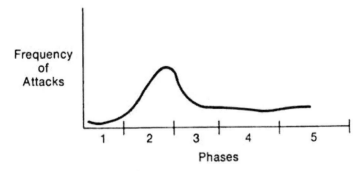

Figure 2. Incidence of attacks on policy.

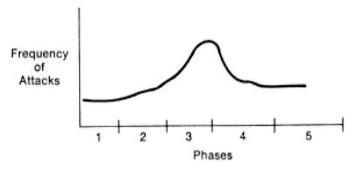

Figure 3. Incidence of attacks on administrative incompetence.

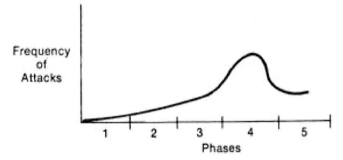

Figure 4. Incidence of attacks for breaking political rules.

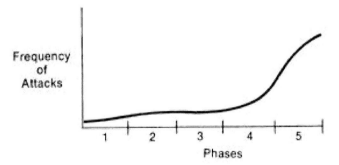

Figure 5. Incidence of personal attacks.

Generalizing the Model

Having developed this degree of confidence in our hypothetical model, let us now see what might be involved in generalizing it beyond the two electoral campaigns used in the test. Two strategies of generalization come to mind:

1. Simple empirical extension. The model could simply be extended to other national elections, state and municipal elections, elections in other countries, and elections in voluntary associations, such as labor unions, to see whether the same regularities hold in the behavior of aspirants to political office. We would, of course, have to modify some of the assumptions and some of the measures according to the different empirical settings.

2. Generalizing the major concepts and reapplying them to non-electoral situations. Suppose we suspect that in generating this model we have uncovered a much more general and fundamental behavioral regularity that applies to many situations other than electoral campaigns and that people's purposive behavior in general will unfold in the following sequence:

Phase 1. Resources are assembled for action (this is a general category, of which the period of quiescence and searching for new modes of attack in an electoral campaign is a special case).

Phase 2. There is a formulation of the *goals* of action (criticism of policies is a special case).

Phase 3. There is a preparation of the *means* to attain goals (attacks on administrative competence is a special case).

Phase 4. There is an assessment of the *norms* that regulate attainment of goals (attacks for breaking the rules of the political game is a special case).

Phase 5. There is an assessment of the *personal qualities* of those who are going to attain the goals (personal attacks on politicians is a special case).

Having generalized the categories of our model in this way, we are now prepared to go to many new kinds of social settings—churches, business firms, families, and so on—and to *respecify* these general categories in terms appropriate for these new settings and to see whether people's purposive, problem-solving behavior unfolds accordingly.

Both methods of generalization—empirical extension and reformulation of concepts—involve the identification of new empirical settings: the first extends the existing variables to directly comparable situations, and the second generalizes the categories so that they can be applied to situations that would not otherwise be thought comparable with electoral campaigns. {6}

What Is Wrong with the Model?

One possible defect in this model is that the data of electoral campaigns simply do not bear out the expectations generated by the model. But for the moment we shall disregard this possible flaw, because we have decided, for purposes of illustration, to use only fake data.

The main inadequacy of the model is that it does not *explain* anything. On the basis of the model we have no reason to know *why* the types of political tactics should have unfolded in the posited sequence. We appear simply to have announced this sequence out of the blue. Thus, the status of the "model" is only that of an empirical generalization about political behavior, not an explanatory theory about it. True, we said that the fact that a party is out of power is an independent (causal) variable, but there is nothing about the quality of "outness" that would explain why the sequence of phases should unfold in a particular order. In short, the most that our model can be is accurately descriptive; it cannot explain.

How can the model be made genuinely explanatory? It must be supplemented by a more general set of postulates and assumptions that would reveal why one set of tactics should precede another in an electoral campaign. Or, to put it more formally, we should have a body of theoretical concepts and propositions from which the sequence could be *derived*. Suppose, for example, we develop the following body of assumptions. Assume that the several tactics can be ranked in terms of possible costs and gains to the out party. On these grounds it is relatively cheap for them to criticize the policies of the party in power, because such attacks, being mild, will not provoke counterattacks from the party in power and will not arouse much internal criticism of tactics within the out party. When, however, opposition political leaders of the out party begin to attack the administrative competence, or even more, the political honesty and personal integrity of the party in power, they provoke retaliatory attacks from the party in power and they provoke criticisms within their own ranks that they are "hitting below the belt." So we have ranked the several tactics both by political potency (their power to discredit the party in power) and by their potential for generating political backlash and disunity within the opposition party.

Assume further that when prospective political gains are remote, opposition parties will balance gains and costs, but minimize risk. However, when the prospective gains are imminent—that is, when the elections get nearer—the opposition continues to seek a balance between political gains and costs, but they are prepared to risk greater losses because the prospects for their gains are nearer at hand. Thus they will be willing to engage in progressively riskier and more extreme tactics as the election approaches.

By thus setting several new variables—gains, costs, and risk—into relationship with one another and by postulating a few psychological assumptions as to how political leaders will maximize their behavior with respect to these variables, we have created some *reasons to expect* that their tactics will unfold in the posited sequence. We have created some theoretical underpinnings for the model, and now we are able to explain why it should be so, rather than merely that it is so. We have not made these underpinnings rigorous enough to say that we have derived the sequence, but we have approached formal derivation. If we had formalized the principles of minimization of cost and maximization of gain into a series of formal postulates, had made risk taking a function of time, and expressed all these relations in mathematical formulas, we could have formally derived a sequence, whereby low-cost, low-gain tactics would gradually give way to high-cost, high-gain tactics over time. This sequence could then have been tested empirically in the ways suggested in the original formulation of the model.

Issues That Arise in Theorizing in the Social Sciences: A General Statement

From this simple model of political behavior—and its weakness—we may now move to a more general statement of the kinds of issues that must be faced by the investigator who proposes to generate a sociological theory. In listing these issues in the order I do, I do not mean to suggest that any one is more important than another, or that the investigator must face the issues in any particular order. What I am saying is that sooner or later he must face all these issues if his theory is to be scientifically complete and he must face them well if his theory is to be scientifically adequate.

Specifying a Problem within a Range of Data

The first problem that arises in the construction of theoretical explanations is to identify what it is we wish to explain. This problem has two aspects: identifying the range of data, and specifying the kind of variation that is problematical. {7}

1. In our political model we specified the tactics of political parties in electoral campaigns as that range of data toward which we wished to direct our attention. To identify this range of data is to say in general what our theory is about. It is a "theory of political tactics."

Sociological models and theory vary greatly in the ranges of data they address. For example, the range of data may be *broad* or *narrow*. An example of a narrow range of data would be found in the theory of a trade cycle designed to explain the temporal movement of several simple, aggregated economic indices—employment, income, and so forth. An example of an extremely broad range of data is Talcott Parsons' "general theory of action," which is explicitly meant to apply to many different kinds of phenomena on many different analytic levels [see page 23]. Or again, the range of data may be *macroscopic* or *microscopic* in its focus. A model designed to predict the sequence of problem-solving activities of an experimental small group is relatively microscopic, whereas a theory designed to explain the nature and workings of industrial society—as in the case of Karl Marx—is macroscopic. Finally, the boundaries of the range of data may be *loosely* or *tightly* defined, depending on the care that the investigator takes in systematically and explicitly excluding phenomena he is not interested in explaining. In our hypothetical model of political tactics, the range of data is relatively narrow because it deals with only a few of many possible aspects of the political process; it is macroscopic because it deals with aggregated aspects of a political system rather than, for example, individual political decision making; and finally, the boundaries of the data are rather tightly defined because it specifies the precise empirical referents of the term "tactics."

A very common shortcoming of theories in the social sciences is that they do not define the relevant range of data with sufficient precision. If we are to think theoretically, it is not permissible to be vaguely interested in "political behavior" or the "political process" in general. It is necessary to specify clearly what aspect or aspects of these general areas are to be addressed. Otherwise we are not prepared to say what phenomena interest us and as a consequence we are not in a position to say precisely what our theory is about.

2. To specify a scientific problem, we select some observed or hypothetical line of variability within the range of data and pose the question, "Why does it vary in the way it does?" In the case of our political model we failed to ask this question in a precise way; instead we asked only how political tactics seem to vary regularly over a period of time. For this reason our theory was bound to be incomplete from the very outset.

Selecting Basic Concepts for Describing and Classifying the Data

Having chosen a range of data for interest and some line of variability for explanation, the theorist must next generate a number of concepts for subdividing the data into appropriate categories so that it can be analyzed. For example, the range of data in our political model is the political tactics of parties. The basic concepts we brought to bear on these data are (1) the subclassification of political tactics into criticizing policy, criticizing administrative incompetence, launching personal attacks on political figures, and so on, and (2) the subclassification of political parties into "ins" and "outs." To apply basic concepts to the data in this way is to slice up the range of data into parts that are appropriate for our purposes of generating a theoretical explanation for the problem we have posed.[5] A different problem might require a different set of concepts to break down the range of data.

One point to remember about the basic concepts in any sociological theory is that they do not have to be identical to the common sense concepts we ordinarily use to think about the empirical world. For example, the first thought that often comes to mind about a political party is "what it stands for" in terms of ideology or "who it stands for" in terms of constituency. In our particular model, we chose an aspect of political parties that might not be quite so close to common sense—that is, whether they did or did not hold office—as the most important determinant of political tactics for our purpose. A second caution is that the basic concepts of a sociological theory do not exhaust reality. They do not identify every aspect of the phenomena we wish to explain. The styles of literature and history are much richer and more nearly complete as descriptions of "reality," considered in its most general sense. In social-scientific theorizing, however, the object is to select from reality particular aspects that are important for explaining the course of specified events. Scientific description is, in short, always selective, never exhaustive of reality. {8}

Finally, it is important to ask: of the multiplicity of concepts available in language, which ones shall we use for purposes of sociological description? Part of the answer to this question lies in the nature of the problem originally posed. For instance, in our model, it seems appropriate to choose the concepts "in" and "out" in connection with explaining the tactics of the parties, because tactics are means a political party uses to try to gain power—that is, to become an "in" party. If we changed the problem, and were attempting to account for the concrete symbols in the party's ideology, the in or out status of the party would probably not be as important; we might wish to turn, instead, to the kind of political constituency from which the party typically draws its support. Another part of the answer depends on how well the theory as a whole works. If our model had turned out to be unverified empirically—that is, if political tactics did not fluctuate in the way we predicted in the model—it may very well have been the case that the choice of in and out status as the major determinant was

---

[5] For a list of typical key concepts in sociology—such as status, role, social distance, and so on—see "The Bearing of Sociological Theory on Empirical Research," in Merton 1968.

not the best one, and other aspects of political life should have been selected.

Specifying Indices or Measures for the Basic Concepts

Thus far we have been dealing mainly in a world of ideas, that is, specifying basic concepts that seem to be important in addressing a given specific problem. In addition, however, we must decide which phenomena in the empirical world constitute indices of these concepts. How do we recognize a political tactic when we see one? How do we recognize an "in" party when we see one? We answered these questions in a relatively simple way. We decided that a given political tactic—for example, an accusation that the party in power was corrupt—had been used when a panel of coders decided that the contents of political reports in *The New York Times* revealed such an accusation. And we decided that a party would be deemed in or out depending on whether it controlled the Presidency. These simple answers are certainly open to criticism. Nevertheless, it still remains one of the central canons of theorizing that empirical indicators—or "operational definitions"—for the basic constructs must be sought. A theory is stronger or weaker according to how adequately this operation is performed.

Organizing the Basic Concepts Logically

To constitute a theory, the basic concepts we have chosen must be more than a simple list. They must be organized logically in relation to one another. Some may be represented as causes, others as effects; some may be represented as logical opposites to others; some may be represented as lying along a continuum. Once these concepts are so organized, a theory may be said to have a *logical structure.* In other words, the concepts may be said to constitute a *theoretical system.* Let me illustrate a few of the issues that arise in considering the logical structure of a theory.

1. *The problem of logical exhaustiveness.* One of the canons that should be observed in constructing a theory is that the basic concepts should cover the entire range of data that is relevant to the scientific problem at hand. The encircled area in figure 6 represents the range

of data, and the subdivided areas represent concepts by which each datum is to be classified.

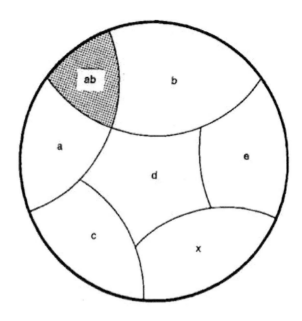

Figure 6. The range of data subdivided by basic concepts.

The rule of logical exhaustiveness says that each datum should be classifiable in terms of the basic concepts. In our political model, for example, it is essential that the range of tactics available to a political party be exhausted by the classification scheme we have devised—attacks on policy, criticisms of administrative competence, and so on (a through e). If this range is not exhausted, we are {9} likely to be confronted with much data on political tactics, the theoretical significance of which we cannot assess.

2. *The problem of residual categories.* Sometimes the range of data is somewhat more complex than that presented in our theory, and while we acknowledge that some items of data fall within the basic range to be studied, we do not wish to treat these items as important. These items of data are assigned to a "residual category" represented as *x*, or non-*abcde*, in figure 6. An example can be provided from our political model. In considering the in and out parties we restricted our attention to the two major parties—Republicans and Democrats. The

world of political parties is, however, much more complicated than this. In every election there are a number of minor parties—for example, Vegetarian, Dixiecrat, Peace and Freedom—that nominate candidates for the Presidency and participate in the electoral campaign. These groups are clearly parties and fall into the range of data subsumed under the general heading "political parties." But for the purposes of our analysis we do not wish to consider them as important, so we create a miscellaneous, or residual, category of "other parties" and consider this category to be nonproblematic for purposes of our model.

The use of residual categories sometimes presents thorny problems. Suppose, in applying our model, we come across the campaigns of 1912 and 1968 in which the third party, headed by Theodore Roosevelt and George Wallace, respectively, played a significant role in the electoral process. Suppose further that our model of the sequence of tactics "fit" the data of the electoral campaign of 1968 but did not fit that of the campaign of 1912. As investigators we would be inclined to say that the campaign of 1912 turned out differently because of the presence of such a powerful third party. Such an interpretation certainly sounds plausible. But in making it, we are creating certain theoretical problems for ourselves. For one thing, we had already decided that "other parties" were theoretically residual—that is, did not play a role in our model—but now we are allowing them to be part of the theory. For another, we appealed to the importance of the third party *selectively*; that is, we have pointed to its importance in 1912, when the data did not come out as predicted, but we are not bothered about it in 1968, when it was as conspicuous in the campaign but did not appear to affect the basic sequence predicted by the model.

The selective use of residual categories is, in short, a way of having our cake and eating it too. On the one hand, we have created a simplified and theoretically rigorous model of political tactics; but on the other hand, we have equipped it with a residual category that we may ignore when we choose and use as an explanation when we choose. It is certainly legitimate to treat "other parties" as an important variable in our theory, if we wish to do so; but if we do, it is necessary to incorporate the concept into the theoretical structure in as logical and consistent a way as the other concepts, rather than rely on it in an ad hoc way. An important task for the theorist is carving clearly defined concepts out of residual concepts and integrating them logically into his theory [Parsons 1949, p. 18].

3. *The problem of mutual exclusiveness.* The canon of mutual exclusiveness says that any item of data should be unequivocally classifiable as an instance of one of the basic concepts. Problems arise when items fall into more than one category—as in the shaded area *ab* in figure 6—because we do not know what kind of theoretical significance to assign them. Suppose, for instance, that in our political model, we made it a condition that in order to be "in" a party had to control both the Presidency and the Congress. In the period 1956-60 (Eisenhower's second term as President), however, the Republicans controlled the Presidency and the Democrats the Congress. Applying our criterion, we would have to say neither party was in power—an absurd result in terms of our model (though perhaps not absurd from other standpoints). Or suppose that the condition for being in is that the party control *either* the Presidency *or* Congress. Between 1956 and 1960 both parties would have been classified as in, also absurd in terms of the model (though again, perhaps not absurd in all senses). Whatever its other merits, our original criterion—control of the Presidency alone—does have the advantage of preventing such absurdities from arising. The conclusion is that the basic concepts of a theory should not overlap logically; and if a questionable instance of classification arises, there should be unambiguous rules for determining how the instance should be classified.

4. *The problem of causal relations.* Perhaps most important, it is essential for the theorist to specify which of his concepts stand for causes and which for effects. (Effects are commonly called dependent variables, causes are called independent variables.) This distinction, above all, is what gives a theory its determinacy and permits the theorist to generate propositions from the theory. In our political model we were rather precise about identifying the effects— {10} there were the different kinds of political tactics. But we were less precise in identifying the causes that might determine the variation in the effects. The original model referred generally to the condition of being "out" as determining the pattern of tactics, but the exact causal mechanism was left rather vague. We attempted to remedy this flaw in the subsequent discussion by involving some psychological generalizations regarding costs, gains, and risks of various political tactics. These generalizations made our model more determinate theo-

retically and permitted us to specify more nearly why the sequence should unfold in a definite pattern.

When we identify causes, we must also identify what kinds of causes they are. Some causes may be represented as necessary conditions; others as triggering mechanisms; others as inhibitors; and still others as intervening between a more remote cause and the ultimate effect. To specify the different kinds of causes and to set them into definite relations with one another gives theory its causal structure.

5. *The problem of "parameters" or "givens."* Any theory must necessarily be selective with respect to both effects and causes. It cannot purport to explain everything in the world, and it cannot incorporate every conceivable cause of the phenomena to be explained. To attempt to do either would lead to an amorphous and unwieldy collection of thousands of variables and relations.

Because a theory selects out certain causes for emphasis, it necessarily makes certain assumptions about what are *not* to be regarded as causes. Consider our model of political tactics. One of the basic unspoken assumptions of that model is that political life takes place in a legal and constitutional structure, within which elections proceed more or less peacefully and by definite procedures. Furthermore, if a constitutional crisis should arise—a constitutional crisis that would jeopardize the entire electoral process—the crisis would certainly have to be reckoned with as a cause that would influence political tactics. But, for purposes of our model, we assumed that there would be no such crisis; we assumed the continuing existence of the constitutional and legal environment of the electoral process. In short, we assumed it to be "given." This assumption that certain potential causes are not operative—that is, "constant" or "given"—is often described as specifying the *parameters* of the theory. Parameters are causes that are known to be potentially important if they vary, but that are assumed, for purposes of constructing a theory, not to vary. As we shall see, we often learn as much about a theory and a theorist by examining the parameters of the theory as we do by examining the operative causes.

Deriving Propositions

Once the logical structure of a theory has been specified, it is possible to generate propositions about the phenomena to be explained by drawing out the logical implications of this structure. This operation is known as *derivation*. Derivation works in the following way: if we make certain assumptions about the parameters and other assumptions about the operative causes and if we organize these causes in a certain way, it follows that the effects will unfold in a certain way. As you will remember, our original model of political tactics lacked a very definite logical structure, so we were unable to derive propositions. Our propositions seemed to be drawn out of thin air. It helped the model—from the standpoint of being able to derive propositions—to supplement it with postulates regarding cost, gain, and risk, because these postulates gave us reasons to predict that the political tactics would unfold in a definite pattern.

Making the Propositions Testable

It is not enough to generate propositions from theory. It is always necessary to return once again to the world of facts and to devise ways of discovering whether our propositions are empirically valid. In our own model, we had to translate the hypothetical sequence of tactics into empirical terms. We had to say how long, in chronological time, a "phase" lasted; we had to specify rules by which changes in tactics could be measured over time; and we had to employ statistical tests to make sure that the changes in the tactics we uncovered could not have happened by chance alone.

One of the most familiar ways of making propositions testable in science is to conduct an experiment. The essence of an experiment is to devise a situation in which all the parameters are held constant, then systematically to vary the causes that are suspected to be operative, in an effort to create the predicted effect. If that effect is created, the proposition is judged to be conditionally verified. Unfortunately, much of the empirical data that are available to social scientists are not experimental data. Ethical and practical considerations prohibit experimenting with some aspects of life; for example, it is not possible to create experimentally a genuine panic in which people might actually be hurt or killed. In {11} addition, much of the data available to social scientists are in the form of historical records, which were recorded, not for purposes of scientific research, but for other purposes. For this reason the social scientist has to rely on methods of testing propositions that are imperfect approximations of the experimental method. For example, he has to hold potential causes constant by means of statistical manipulation or by means of comparative illustration. As we shall see, the theorists we have chosen for examination vary greatly in the manner in which they attempt to make their general propositions empirically testable.

Testing the Propositions

The final question to be asked of a theory is whether the specified empirical data do or do not conform to the propositions generated from the conceptual structure of the theory. If they conform—as we made our data do in the model of political tactics—the appropriate scientific strategy is tentatively to accept the proposition as valid and to attempt to extend the theory empirically and conceptually.

Suppose, however, the data do not conform to theoretical expect-ations. In this case a number of strategies are available to us. We may reexamine the data to see that we measured and coded it properly. We may invent new indices for the theory and attempt to test it on them. We may change our rules for locating operational definitions for the basic concepts. Or, alternatively, we may decide that the data are perfectly adequate, reliable, and valid, but that the theory is inadequate. We may suspect that we identified the wrong variables as causes and that we should create a new model with different fun-damental causes. Or it may be that we had created an inappropriate causal structure, and it is necessary to reconceptualize the nature of the causal relations in the theory. Finally, it may be that certain of our parametric assumptions were erroneous, and it is necessary to modify some of these. One way of putting the matter is this: there is only one way for a theory to be right, and that is if all the issues involved in generating and testing the theory have been effectively met; but there are many different ways in which it can be wrong.

One bad habit that frequently tempts theorists when the data do not conform to theoretical expectations is to fall back on residual categories to account for apparent exceptions. In testing the model of political tactics, for example, suppose that I found that in the 1936-1940 electoral period personal attacks on the President ran very high throughout all four years of the electoral campaign, thus appearing to disconfirm our prediction that these attacks would cluster just before the election. Faced with this discrepancy, suppose I had attempted to account for it by asserting that President Roosevelt's personality was such that it provoked especially strong reactions. To fall back on this new variable—"the President's personality"—as an explanation is to resort to a factor that was not originally incorporated in the theory. To do this, furthermore, is to fail to confront the fact that the theory, as originally formulated, did not fit the facts. It is a way of letting a theory bend without forcing it to break. By relying on residual categories in this way, the theorist is likely to give the impression that the theory simultaneously covers a great range of data *and* has a rigorous logical structure. But in reality this habit involves a sacrifice of logical structure, because the special, or residual, category involved has not been incorporated into the logical structure in the first place. To put it another way, a theory should be able to be falsified; but if it is surrounded by a number of residual categories that can be called upon whenever the theory appears to be embarrassed by facts that do not fit it, the theory cannot be proved wrong. I mention this habit in particular because we shall find it practiced in various ways by the several theorists whose work we are going to examine.

Concluding Remarks

Many controversies have arisen in the history of philosophy and the history of science around the issues of theory versus facts and deduction versus induction as the proper way to generate knowledge. The preceding discussion of the issues that must be faced in theorizing suggests that some aspects of these controversies have not been fruitful. To my mind, the operations of moving from facts to theories (induction) and from theories to facts (deduction) are not competitors in the race for knowledge. The generation of scientific knowledge involves a constant interplay between both types of operations—a constant process of creating propositions from concepts and theories, and a constant process of rejecting, confirming, or modifying these propositions in the light of empirical data. It is possible to err in moving from theoretical concepts to empirical research, and it is possible to err in moving back again. But both activities are necessary for the generation of scientific explanations. {12}

Having set forth the issues that are faced in the generation of theory, and having specified some of the desiderata for facing these issues, we are now prepared to turn to the work of several social theorists. We shall use the foregoing discussion as a scaffolding, as a framework for summarizing, criticizing, and in some cases reformulating the works of these theorists. I have chosen theorists who thought, at least implicitly, about many of these issues. Not all of them faced all the issues; and they did not face them equally well. Thus the several theories differ in their degree of theoretical adequacy. By examining major sociological theories in this framework, we not only arrive at a notion of the adequacy of each, but hopefully we shall also sharpen our critical faculties in approaching other theories in the social sciences.

Émile Durkheim's Theory of Suicide

Durkheim's purposes in undertaking his classic work on suicide were many. He was attempting to refute psychological, biological, and physical theories of social phenomena and to insist on the importance of distinctively social explanations for social facts, such as suicide rates.[6] And in insisting on the importance of social cohesion as an important determinant in social life in *Suicide* and other works, he assumed a polemic position contrary to other sociological theories, such as the individualistic theory of Herbert Spencer and the materialistic theory of Karl Marx.[7] In this essay, however, we shall not consider these kinds of purposes in any detail, important as they may be; rather, we shall treat Durkheim's work as an effort to create a sociological theory of suicide and examine how he faced the problems that confronted him in this enterprise.

---

[6] For Durkheim's own statement on his methodological position, see chapter 5 of *The Rules of the Sociological Method*, published two years before the appearance of *Suicide*.

[7] For Durkheim's polemic against Spencer, see chapter 7 of Book One in *The Division of Labor in Society*; see also pp. 311ff. of Parsons' *The Structure of Social Action*. For an attempt to uncover the relations between the work of Durkheim and Marx, see Zeitlin 1968, chapter 15.

A Selective Summary of Durkheim's Theory

The range of data and the problem. Put most simply, Durkheim was interested in accounting for variations in rates of suicide among different social groups, as these variations were revealed in the statistics available in the 1890's. Most of these statistics came from European countries, but he did have limited information on other societies as well. In one respect Durkheim's starting point was an advantageous one. His range of data was fairly well delimited, and the statistics, however unreliable they might be, were available in the official records of many countries.

In identifying this problem, Durkheim insisted that he was not concerned with suicide as an individual phenomenon. Rather, he was concerned with differences in rates of suicide—why the proportion of suicides among businessmen was higher than the proportion of suicides among workers, for example. Furthermore, in his search for causes of suicide, he also emphasized the social. While acknowledging a wide range of causes of suicide, he proposed not to concern himself with "the individual as such, his motives and his ideas," but to concentrate on the influences of "various social environments (religious confessions, family, political society, occupational groups, etc.)" [p. 151].[8]

Durkheim was also careful to define his topic of interest clearly and to set it off from other, related phenomena. He defined suicide as "all cases of death resulting directly or indirectly from a positive or negative act of the victim himself which he knows will produce this result" [p. 44]. On the basis of this definition he excluded suicide of animals, which, he felt, could not know the consequences of their actions, and the suicides of the victims of hallucination. The definetion also permitted him to draw at least an approximate line between suicide in its full sense and the deaths of alcoholics, daredevils, and scholars who work themselves to death. Durkheim felt it important to

---

[8] In fact, Durkheim felt that the individual "motives" or "reasons" given for suicide—personal sorrow, economic hardship, and so on—were unhelpful in understanding suicide as a social phenomenon [pp. 148-50]. (The page references in brackets in this section refer to the English edition of *Suicide* [published by the Free Press].)

define suicide in this way, and not in terms of motives or ends, which were difficult to discover and assess.[9]

Basic concepts. Before recounting Durkheim's social explanation of suicide, it is necessary to analyze in more detail his conception of suicide and its causes as *social facts.* He mobilized a variety of arguments to demonstrate the value of this conception.

First, arguing by elimination, he attempted to show that explanations relying on factors other than the {13} social one are inadequate. For example, he ruled out individual insanity as a cause of suicides. In doing so, he used both definitional and empirical arguments. On definitional grounds he argued that there are many instances of types of suicide that do not display the same mental characteristics that insanity does [pp. 62-67]. On empirical grounds he employed the following kinds of arguments. (1) More women than men are found in the populations of insane asylums. But the suicide rate in the society at large expresses the opposite ratio. For this reason insanity appears not to be associated with suicide [pp. 71-72]. (2) Similarly, insanity rates seem to reach a peak about age 35, remain constant to about age 60, and decline thereafter. But suicide "increases regularly from childhood to the most advanced old age" [p. 73], suggesting again that insanity is an unlikely cause of suicide.[10]

With respect to alcoholism as a possible cause, Durkheim compared maps of France, one showing the distribution of alcoholism and the other showing the distribution of suicide rates. Noting that the two phenomena clustered in very different ways, he concluded that alcoholism could not be regarded as an adequate explanation of suicide [pp. 77-78]. Using similar types of arguments, he attempted to push aside every cause he could find—heredity, weather, race, and so forth—thus creating a presumption, in favor of his preferred cause, the social factor.

---

[9] Here Durkheim displayed his "positivistic" preference for identifiable "facts" and his predilection to avoid investigation of inaccessible mental states [p. 43].

[10] These arguments are likely to strike us as weak and somewhat quaint. Their weakness lies in that Durkheim was relying on the highly unsatisfactory psychological concepts of his day, in that he was arguing on the basis of very poor data relating to both insanity and suicide, and in that he was using associations between aggregated social data as evidence for statements about psychological mechanisms.

To argue by elimination only, however, has inherent limitations, for no matter how effectively other causes are refuted, the positive importance of the social factor is not yet established by direct evidence. Durkheim was aware of this point, and devoted most of his energy to a positive demonstration of the importance of social determinants. Initially, he developed a number of general arguments. He noted, for example, that suicide rates for any given society are almost invariant from year to year. He also noted that total mortality rates fluctuate more than suicide rates in a society from year to year. To Durkheim these two observations suggested that some general *social* feature of the society—or what we might call "national character"—was responsible for the remarkable stability of suicide rates. And by comparing the large and persistent differences among countries such as Italy (low suicide rate) and Denmark (high suicide rate), he concluded that a definite suicide rate is "peculiar to each social group where it can be considered as a characteristic index" [p. 50]. On the basis of such arguments, Durkheim insisted that a new order of fact, a social fact, had to be brought to bear on our understanding of differences in suicide rates. This type of fact possesses a reality of its own, and its own distinctive characteristics.

So much for Durkheim's general case. But to insist on the *general* importance of the social factor does not generate very specific propositions about variations in suicide rates. To do this, Durkheim identified social cohesion as an especially salient factor in the etiology of suicide. As employed by Durkheim, the notion of cohesion refers to the ways in which individuals are attached to the collective values of the community and the ways in which individual needs and desires are regulated by normative expectations.

Durkheim identified four types of social cohesion that are most relevant to the understanding of the causes of suicide:

1. Egoism.   Normally, egoism refers to the gratification of self-interest, or selfishness. Durkheim preferred to give the term a primarily social meaning, though he did retain a thread of its psychological meaning. For him, egoism refers to the social condition in which individual activities take precedence over collective allegiances and obligations. Under this condition men become detached from the bonds of collective life and become the masters of their own destinies.

2. Altruism.   The opposite of egoism, this term refers to the condition in which man is insufficiently individuated from collective

obligations and, as a result, has little control over his destiny. Altruism encompasses phenomena such as loyalty, honor, commitment, self-sacrifice for the greater social good, and the like.

3. Anomie. The literal meaning of this term is "rulelessness" or "without regulation." Normally, Durkheim argued, society plays an important regulative role in the life of an individual. Through normative systems of justice, equity, and distribution, the society controls and regulates his needs and desires. Under conditions of social stability, moreover, man's life experiences—his pleasures, his disappointments—conform more or less to the expectations established by the regulative norms of society. Under conditions of sudden crisis or drastic social change, however, individuals' life experiences diverge sharply from what the norms governing their lives have led them to expect, and this makes for a discontinuity in social regulation. The result is anomie. {14}

4. Fatalism. Durkheim included the fourth type of suicide mainly for completeness' sake and did not develop it. The opposite of anomie, fatalism refers to excessive normative regulation and occurs when "futures [are] pitilessly blocked and passions violently choked by oppressive discipline" [p. 276].

Indices for the basic concepts. With respect to identifying his dependent variable—the rate of suicide—Durkheim referred to official statistics and to various impressionistic accounts of suicide for different societies. For several reasons such data are quite unreliable,[11] so the conclusions Durkheim drew from them must be tempered with appropriate skepticism. Nevertheless, these were the only statistics available to Durkheim, and certainly better than no data at all.

With respect to empirical instances of the major types of social integration, Durkheim proceeded as follows:

1. Egoism. Durkeim found illustrations of egoistic integration in the religious, the familial, and the political spheres. Protestantism is an example of an egoistic religion, because of its antiauthoritarianism, its emphasis on the individual's direct relations to God, and its tradition of free inquiry—all of which detach men from their social environment. By contrast, Catholicism would be less egoistic, because it

---

[11] For a brief review of some of the questions that have been raised about suicide statistics, see George Simpson's "Editor's Introduction" to *Suicide* [pp. 17-20].

has more common beliefs, a more doctrinaire approach, and a more authoritarian tradition than Protestantism [pp. 157-159]. Finally, Judaism would rank lowest on egoism, since it, "like all early religions, consists basically of a body of practices minutely governing all the details of life and leaving little free room to individual judgment" [p. 160].

For the familial sphere, Durkheim maintained that unmarried and widowed persons are more detached from domestic society than married persons, and that persons in small families are relatively more detached than those in large families.

Finally, for the political sphere, Durkheim argued that egoism decreases during episodes of political turmoil, such as war and revolutionary crisis.

> Great social disturbances and great popular wars rouse collective sentiments, stimulate partisan spirit and patriotism, political and national faith, alike, and concentrating activity toward a single end, at least temporarily cause a stronger integration of society.... As they force men to close ranks and confront the common danger, the individual thinks less of himself and more of the common cause [p. 208].

2. Altruism. Most of Durkheim's illustrations of altruism are found in travelers' and ethnographers' accounts of certain primitive societies, in which the burdens of custom were excessive, and other societies noted for their high degree of social integration, such as classical Japan and classical India. But his most consistent and most thorough illustrations were found in the military systems, particularly those organized around values of honor, loyalty, and obedience.

3. Anomie. The illustrations of anomie came mainly from the economic and familial spheres. One feature of economic life that is particularly conducive to anomie is the business crisis. Even those of us who do not personally remember the Great Crash of 1929 still conjure up in our minds the image of the businessman who took his life after being wiped out financially. For Durkheim, however, the business crash is anomie, not because the individual loses his fortune, but because he becomes disoriented: what he has come to expect is no longer available to him.

By the same token, Durkheim argued that a business boom creates a condition of anomie, because it, like the crash, upsets the relationship between man's expectations and his life experiences. It stimulates insatiable desires that cannot be quenched as his fortunes come to outstrip his expectations. Both crises of depression and crises of prosperity, in short, are "disturbances of the collective order" [p. 246]. Human activity is released from all restraint, and "nothing in the world can enjoy such a privilege" [p. 252].

In the familial sphere Durkheim considered divorce to be a prime example of anomie. Viewing marriage as "a regulation of sexual relations, including not merely the physical instincts which this intercourse involves but the feelings of every sort gradually engrafted by civilization on the foundation of physical desire" [p. 270], he regarded divorce as weakening this kind of regulation and, consequently, releasing unmanageable passions and desires.

4. Fatalism. Here Durkheim's illustrations are sparse. Perhaps the clearest example of fatalism would be the social condition of the slave, as well as others who live under excessive and despotic rules, "against which there is no appeal" [p. 276].

Logical relations among the basic concepts. By now it is clear that Durkheim was not dealing with a simple, unorganized list of causes and effects in relation to suicide. The several types of cohesion (egoism, altruism, anomie, fatalism) are independent variables, the suicide rate dependent. Furthermore, the four types constitute two sets of paired opposites. {15}

Egoism is a condition of too great detachment of the individual from the community, altruism a condition of too little detachment; anomie is a condition of too little regulation by normative expectations, fatalism is a condition of too great regulation. Such is the basic structure of Durkheim's theoretical system.

A number of additional variables—sometimes only implicit—arise when we consider the mechanisms that link the various types of cohesion with suicide. With respect to altruistic suicide, for example, suicide occurs as a result of conformity to group values:

> Either death [has] to be imposed by society as a duty, or
> some question of honor [is] involved, or at least some
> disagreeable occurrence [has] to lower the value of life in
> the victim's eyes . . . it even happens that the individual

kills himself purely for the joy of sacrifice, because, even with no particular reason, renunciation in itself is considered praiseworthy [p. 223].

With respect to egoistic religious suicide, however, another type of mechanism is involved. The individual is not directly encouraged to take his life. Indeed, as Durkheim noted, both Protestantism and Catholicism have strong taboos against suicide [p. 157]. The essential difference is that Protestantism encourages free inquiry, thus throwing the individual more on his own resources, less protected by group solidarity; in contrast, Catholicism puts less emphasis on individual conscience, encourages expiation of guilt through the confessional, and the like [pp. 157-158]. The mechanism whereby Protestantism encourages suicide, then, is a by-product, not a direct result, of conformity with the specific values of the Protestant religion.

The other types of egoistic suicide involve still other mechanisms. Speaking of the importance of large family size as a deterrent to suicide, Durkheim seemed to think that the "social density" as such was an important integrative mechanism:

> Where collective sentiments are strong, it is because the force with which they affect each individual conscience is echoed in all the others, and reciprocally. The intensity they attain therefore depends on the number of consciences which react to them in common. For the same reason, the larger the crowd, the more capable of violence the passions vented by it. Consequently, in a family of small numbers, common sentiments and memories cannot be very intense; for there are not enough consciences in which they can be represented and reenforced by sharing them [p. 202].

In connection with egoism in the political sphere, Durkheim stressed the presence of a common foe in building solidarity and high morale, thus protecting the individual against the possibility of self-destruction. And finally, with respect to anomic suicide, he felt that lack of regulation had the psychological effect of confusing and disorienting the individual, thus making him more vulnerable to all kinds of passions and more prone to self-destruction.

Evidently, then, Durkheim acknowledged, sometimes explicitly and sometimes implicitly, that the social determinants of suicide excite psychological forces in the individual, which in turn manifest themselves in the act of suicide. At one point in his analysis he argued that the social factors do not act in the same way on all individuals: "Each victim of suicide gives his act a personal stamp which expresses his temperament, the special conditions in which he is involved, and which, consequently, cannot be explained by the social and general causes of the phenomenon" [pp. 277-278]. Nevertheless, Durkheim was convinced that the social causes made a "collective mark" on individuals. The typical individual expression of the social state of egoism, for example, is a "loathness to act" and a "melancholy detachment." Egoistic suicides also have an "intellectual and meditative nature" because of the "high development of knowledge and reflective intelligence" in egoistic persons [pp. 278-283].

Thus, even though Durkheim insisted on constructing a relatively simple theoretical system of social variables to explain the suicide rate, he actually supplemented this structure by introducing a number of different psychological assumptions that made the link between the different forms of cohesion and the social incidence of suicide intelligible. These psychological assumptions are, moreover, in the nature of "residual categories" because Durkheim did not incorporate them systematically into his theory.

Generation of hypotheses. Our discussion of the logical structure of Durkheim's theoretical scheme has already revealed his master hypothesis: extremes of social cohesion—too much and too little—cause high suicide rates. Since he specified two dimensions of cohesion—integration and regulation—this master hypothesis breaks down into four versions. With respect to integration, egoism and altruism both make for high suicide rates, with a lower rate falling between the two extremes, where individual interests and collective interests are more or less evenly balanced. Figure 7 represents these relationships graphically. A similar set of hypotheses is generated for the dimension of regulation, with anomie and fatalism the extremes that cause high suicide rates, with intermediate conditions making for lower rates. {16}

Figure 7. Egoism, altruism, and the suicide rate.

Making the hypotheses testable. Having specified the relations among a number of theoretical variables and having identified a number of empirical instances of these variables, the problem of testing the emergent hypotheses is a fairly straightforward matter. If the hypotheses are to be confirmed, Protestants should have higher rates of suicide than Catholics, and Catholics higher than Jews. Single persons should be more prone to suicide than married persons, and married persons without children more prone to suicide than married persons with children. The suicide rate should drop during revolutionary and wartime crises and rise as these crises come to a close. Military personnel should commit suicide at a higher rate than civilians. Economic crises of all sorts should show a rise in the suicide rate. Divorced persons should show higher suicide rates than those in other marital categories. And so on down the line for the various forms of social cohesion.

Testing the hypotheses. To test the relations that emerge from his theory, Durkheim assembled the available data and attempted to demonstrate that the various social groupings and social categories identified in his theory showed the kinds of differences in suicide rates that are predicted in the theory. Table 1, showing consistent differences between Protestants and Catholics, is a typical statistical presentation used by Durkheim.

On the face of it, most of Durkheim's statistical information points in the directions suggested by his hypotheses. This is not to say, however, that his theory should be pronounced as empirically valid on the basis of his evidence alone. The following are a sample of the

Table 1. Suicides in Different Countries per Million by Religious Persuasion

		Protestants:	Catholics:
Austria	(1852-59)	79.5	51.3
Prussia	(1849-55)	159.9	49.6
Prussia	(1869-72)	187	69
Prussia	(1890)	240	100
Baden	(1852-62)	139	117
Baden	(1870-74)	171	136.7
Baden	(1878-88)	242	170
Bavaria	(1844-56)	135.4	49.1
Bavaria	(1884-91)	224	94
Wurttemberg	(1846-60)	113.5	77.9
Wurttemberg	(1873-76)	190	120
Wurttemberg	(1881-90)	170	119

Source: Adapted from Table XVII [Durkheim 1897, p. 154].

kinds of questions Durkheim's critics have raised with respect to his data and the inferences he drew from them:

1. The data, drawn mainly from municipal and provincial archives, were irregularly recorded, and Durkheim had no way of knowing the ways in which they might have been biased in the recording process. For example, were Catholic suicides consistently underreported because of the especially strong stigma attached to suicide among Catholics?

2. While many of Durkheim's basic findings—concerning the relations between age, sex, marital status, and religion on the one side and suicide on the other—have stood the test of subsequent research quite well, more recent and improved data have indicated that some of the empirical relations posited by him do not hold. Andrew Henry and James F. Short, for example, compiled extensive—and more recent—statistics on the changes in the suicide rate in relation to business indices and found that while suicide rates do rise during periods of economic slump, they drop—contrary to Durkheim's assertion—during periods of economic prosperity [Henry & Short

1954]. Such findings, if valid, raise questions, not only about Durkheim's data, but about the psychological assumptions he incorporated into his explanation of anomic suicide.

3. Many of Durkheim's empirical associations involve the "ecological fallacy." For example, to point out that the Bavarian provinces with Protestant majorities have a higher suicide rate than Bavarian provinces with Catholic majorities [p. 153] in no way demonstrates that Protestants commit suicide in the former and Catholics commit suicide in the latter. To confirm the relation, Durkheim would have had to demonstrate an association between religious preference and suicide at the level of individual persons, not simply at the province level. The general point is this: on the basis of ecological associations between two characteristics in the larger units (provinces in this case), it is not possible to infer causal relations between the characteristics for smaller units (individual persons in this case).[12]

In some cases an empirical claim made by Durkheim is not actually evident in the statistics on which he based the claim. For example, in one statistical {17} table comparing the suicide rates of Protestants, Catholics, and Jews in different countries for different periods, Jews showed *higher* suicide rates than Catholics in six of twelve cases [p. 154]. Such a finding should cast some doubt on the posited relation between the two religious groups with respect to suicide, but Durkheim continued to maintain that "the aptitude of Jews for suicide is . . . in a very general way . . . though to a lesser degree, lower than that of Catholics" [p. 155]. True, Durkheim did attempt to adduce reasons why the differences between Catholics and Jews were not greater than the statistics showed—for example, that Jews live in cities and are in intellectual occupations, and therefore are inclined to suicide for reasons other than their religion [p. 155]. But in many instances the reasons seem either forced or unsubstantiated except by logic.[13]

In fairness to Durkheim on this point, it should be pointed out that he sometimes used relatively sophisticated methods to isolate

---

[12] A discussion of the ecological fallacy in *Suicide* is found in Selvin 1958.

[13] Whitney Pope [1970] has undertaken a most detailed examination of the statistical basis for the inferences in *Suicide* and has concluded that in some cases Durkheim did not bring data that were neutral or disconfirmatory to bear on his arguments.

causal forces. For example, he frequently undertook further analysis to establish the validity of a suspected association. On examining the countries on which religious data were available, for example, Durkheim noticed that in most cases Catholics were in the minority. Could it not be, he asked, that minority status rather than religious tradition is the operative variable in the genesis of lower suicide rates among Catholics? To throw light on this question, he examined regions such as Austria and Bavaria, where Catholics are in the majority; in these regions he discovered some diminution of the religious differences between Protestants and Catholics, but Protestant rates were still higher. On the basis of this examination, he concluded that "Catholicism does not . . . owe [its protective influence] solely to its minority status" [p. 157]. In this operation Durkheim was making minority status into a constant in order to isolate the distinctive influence of the religious variable. In comparing military and civilian suicides, and in comparing suicides of married and single persons, Durkheim frequently held age and sex constant in order better to isolate the effect of military and marital status.

Another device that Durkheim used to strengthen his inferences was to replicate general findings at different levels. With respect to altruistic suicide, he predicted higher rates of suicide among military personnel than among civilians, and the available suicide statistics tended to support this hypothesis. It might be argued, however, that on the basis of this gross comparison alone it is not clear that Durkheim had isolated the salient differences between military and civilian personnel; after all, they differed in many other circumstances than in degree of commitment to a code of honor. To support his interpretation, Durkheim turned to the analysis of *intramilitary* differences in suicide rates. First, he compared those with limited terms of service with those of longer duration, finding that the latter— presumably more imbued with the military spirit than the former— showed higher suicide rates. Next, he compared officers and non-commissioned officers with private soldiers, finding the former— again more involved in the military life—showing higher rates. Finally, he found a greater tendency for suicide among volunteers and re-enlisted men, that is, those who chose the military life freely, than among conscripts. Summarizing these findings, Durkheim concluded that "the members of the army most stricken by suicide are also those who are most inclined to this career. . . [p. 233]. By this replication *within* the military Durkheim rendered most plausible the relation *between* military and civilian personnel.[14]

Some Conceptual and Theoretical Problems

From our hasty examination of Durkheim's use of empirical data, we may conclude that while Durkheim exercised care and ingenuity in interpreting his statistical data, the quality of the data and some of his own inferences call for caution in accepting some of his results as definitive. We shall not pursue this conclusion further, mainly because we are concerned more with the logic of theorizing rather than with research design and empirical inference in this essay. Let us turn, then, to a number of theoretical problems in Durkheim's work.

A definitional problem. As indicated, Durkheim approached suicide from a positivistic point of view. He wanted to conceptualize suicide, not in terms of a mental state, but as a tangible act, which could be identified and measured. For this reason he eschewed defining it by reference to motives or "ends sought by the actor." His positivism also is expressed in his own definition of suicide: "all cases of death resulting directly or indirectly from a positive or negative act of the victim himself, which he knows will produce this result." {18}

While Durkheim's definition appears to be relatively straightforward, closer examination raises a number of questions. First, it is not clear that Durkheim actually avoided reference to "internal states" of the individual, hard as he tried to do so. In fact his definition requires that the victim "know that the act will produce this result." Even though this is a cognitive criterion, it is no less "internal" to the actor than a motive. Moreover, such knowledge is often very difficult to establish,[15] especially since the victim cannot report on his state of mind after the act of suicide. It appears, then, that Durkheim's own definition is not entirely consistent with his positivistic stance.

---

[14] For an examination of Durkheim's approximations to multivariate analysis, as well as replication, see Selvin 1958.

[15] Durkheim himself was aware that the knowledge that death would result is difficult to establish, as his discussion of the relations between pure suicide and the deaths of the heroic soldier, the daredevil, etc., indicate [pp. 45-46].

Some ambiguities in Durkheim's basic categories. While our earlier discussion indicated that egoism, altruism, anomie, and fatalism could be represented as two sets of paired opposites on the dimensions of integration and regulation, a closer examination of the ways in which Durkheim employed these variables suggests that their relations to one another are fraught with ambiguity.

Consider egoism first. Its essence appears to lie in the degree of detachment from group life. But as Durkheim's discussion developed, a number of different possible meanings arose. With respect to religious egoism, he referred to the commitment to values of individualism and freedom that isolate the individual from the group; with respect to familial egoism, he referred to a kind of quantitative social density, or frequency of interaction among numbers of persons; and with respect to political egoism, he referred to closeness arising from common commitment to a collectivity facing an external threat.

This multiplicity of meanings of egoism raises the question of whether that concept should stand in paired opposition to altruism. Altruism appears to be opposite only to the first, religious meaning of egoism; religious egoism is primarily a lack of commitment to dogma, whereas altruism is unquestioning faith. Altruism may also stand in opposition to "lack of common commitment under external threat." But it is difficult to ascertain the sense in which altruism is opposite to "lack of social density" in some quantitative sense.

Even Durkheim's discussion of religious egoism is ambiguous. In contrasting Protestantism and Catholicism, two possible readings of religious egoism emerge. The first, stemming from Durkheim's argument that Protestantism is not a doctrinaire religion, suggests that egoism means that individuals are less collectively bound to values and thus are more detached from society. But a second meaning of Protestantism is that individuals are strongly bound to values such as free inquiry; in fact, the more strongly they adhere to these values, the more likely they are to pursue their individual ends. On the one hand, Durkheim appears to argue that the weakness of attachment to values encourages high suicide rates among Protestants. In this case egoism would be the opposite of altruism. Yet on the other hand he appears to argue that strong attachment to certain *kinds* of values—such as liberty, free inquiry, and the like—encourages suicide. In this case egoism and altruism would not be all that different.

Thus egoism and altruism, as defined and used by Durkheim, do not seem to be paired opposites on the dimension of social integration, but instead conceal a more complicated series of dimensions, the exact relations among which are not specified. Even if a satisfactory opposition between the two could be established, however, another fundamental problem remains. In Durkheim's discussion of egoism, he ranked Protestantism, Catholicism, and Judaism in diminishing levels of egoism, with Judaism, "like all early religions," the most integrated of all, hence the most protected against suicide. But in discussing altruistic suicide, he argued that other early religions, such as the Japanese, the Indian, and various primitive religions, were so demanding of the individual that they encouraged altruistic suicide. These assertions leave Judaism with an ambiguous theoretical status. Should it be considered "unegoistic" in contrast to Protestantism and therefore protective against individual self-destruction, or should it be considered "altruistic," like other early religions, and thus encouraging suicide? Or, to put the question more generally, where does the diminishing egoism end and where does increasing altruism begin? Unless the dimension of integration is represented as a scale, with definite intervals to which cases can be assigned, it is possible to characterize almost any empirical instance as either egoistic or altruistic, depending on the other empirical instances with which it is being compared.

With respect to anomie, too, Durkheim's analysis is ambiguous. On the one hand, he characterized anomie as a sudden discontinuity between life experiences and established normative expectations, as in the cases of business crises and divorce. On the other hand, he characterized anomie as a "regular, constant {19} factor," indeed a "chronic state" in trade and industry [p. 254], which he regarded as relatively unregulated by traditional religious and political norms. Out of this chronic lack of regulation arises a kind of chronic state of crisis, restlessness, unbounded ambitiousness, and futility [p. 256].

Given the multiplicity of meanings of both egoism and anomie, the differences between these two concepts also become unclear. Durkheim himself recognized the overlap in meaning when he acknowledged that "both [anomic and egoistic suicide] spring from society's insufficient presence in individuals." But he also insisted that the two differ on both the social and individual level. For egoistic suicide, society is "deficient in truly collective activity, thus depriving the latter of object and meaning"; for anomic suicide, "society's influence is lacking in the basically individual passions, thus leaving them without a check-rein" [p. 258]. On the individual level,

> Suicides of both [egoistic and anomic] types suffer from what has been called the disease of the infinite. But the disease does not assume the same form in both cases. In [egoistic suicide], reflective intelligence is affected and immoderately overnourished; in [anomic suicide], emotion is overexcited and freed from all restraint. In one, thought, by dint of falling back upon itself, has no object left; in the other, passion, no longer recognizing bounds, has no goal left. The former is lost in the infinity of dreams, the second in the infinity of desires [p. 287].

Despite his insistence on their independence, however, his descriptions are so vague and general that it becomes difficult to know when to classify a given social situation as egoistic or anomic, or both.[16]

The implication of these criticisms is that, although Durkheim presented his theory of suicide as a simple, compact, and logically coherent theoretical scheme, it is in fact something of a jumble of ambiguous and only partially interrelated variables. It is wanting in logical structure and, as a consequence, wanting in the ability to generate consistent propositions. It is as though Durkheim, presented with a great array of empirical differences in suicide rates among a number of social groups and social categories, subtly changed the meaning of a number of general terms—terms such as egoism, anomie, and so on—in order to render these empirical results plausible and consistent. But in doing so he damaged his theory by sacrificing some of its logical structure.

Durkheim's use of "floating" and residual categories. To loosen the logical structure of a theory renders it less able to generate propositions, since the relations among the basic categories are no longer fixed. For the same reason, to loosen the logical structure also permits the investigator to use variables in a number of ad hoc ways to account for apparent exceptions to the theory. Durkheim sometimes used his major categories in a somewhat arbitrary or "floating" way

---

[16] A more detailed examination of the conceptual overlap between egoism and anomie led Barclay Johnson [1965] to conclude that the two concepts should, for all intents and purposes, be treated as identical and therefore as a single variable.

and also tended to rely on a number of residual categories that were not "officially" incorporated in his theory.

For instance, consider Durkheim's discussion of the role of education in the etiology of suicide. In contrasting suicide rates among various religious groupings, he argued that free inquiry, as nourished by Protestantism, gives rise to an emphasis on education. "When irrational beliefs or practices have lost their hold [as among Protestants], appeal must be made, in the search for others, to the enlightened consciousness of which knowledge is only the highest form." Thus, he continued, the decline of religious doctrine and the valuation of education "are one and spring from the same source" [p. 162]. He then proceeded to show in varying ways that level of education is positively correlated with suicide rates.

At this point, however, Durkheim noted "one case . . . in which our law [relating education to suicide] might seem not to be verified." This case was Judaism, which "counts the fewest suicides, yet in none other is education so general" [p. 167]. In fact, Durkheim identified precisely the opposite correlation between education and suicide for Jews from that which he found among the Protestants. How did he interpret this apparent exception? He argued that the Jew, who has lived as a member of an embattled minority for centuries, "seeks to learn, not in order to replace his collective prejudices by reflective thought, but merely to be better armed for the struggle" [p. 168]. He maintained, in short, that the *significance* of religion is different for Protestants and for Jews.

In this assertion Durkheim may have been empirically correct. But his shifting of ground underscores the looseness of his theoretical scheme. Explaining education among Protestants as a manifestation of free inquiry—one meaning of egoism—he shifted his argument for Jews, maintaining that the emphasis on education is in fact a manifestation of *another* facet of egoism, namely, the degree to which a group is in a state of political crisis. The Jews, argued Durkheim, have been in a kind of chronic state of political crisis, and this has affected both their interest in education {20} and their low rate of suicide. But the fact that egoism has a number of meanings permitted Durkheim to appeal to one facet of the variable when the statistics fell one way, and to another facet when they fell another way. To shift from meaning to meaning in this way permits the investigator to be right all the time, but at the same time his theory begins to develop another short-coming, lack of falsifiability.[17]

In other instances, Durkheim appealed to variables foreign to his main theoretical framework. The impact of sex on the propensity to suicide is a conspicuous example. In a long and somewhat tortured passage in a chapter on egoistic suicide, Durkheim attempted to sort out some apparently contradictory statistics on the effect of marriage and widowhood on suicide by arguing that the "most favored sex" in each society is protected more from suicide by marriage and widow-hood [pp. 178-189]. In another passage, in which he was attempting to account for the fact that men seem more adversely affected by divorce in societies in which divorce is common, he posed the following, somewhat quaint explanation:

> Woman's sexual needs have less of a mental character [than man's] because, generally speaking, her mental life is less developed. These needs are more closely related to the needs of the organism, following rather than leading them, and consequently find in them an efficient restraint. Being a more instinctive creature than man, woman has only to follow her instincts to find calmness and peace [p. 272].

Perhaps we should generously write off the substance of Durkheim's observation on sexual differences as reflecting the late Victorian prejudices of his day. From the standpoint of his theoretical account of suicide, however, it is apparent that Durkheim was appealing to a factor—innate sexual differences—that was extraneous to his main explanatory framework to account for facts on which the basic variables themselves threw little or no light. The apparently arbitrary use of categories such as these contributes further to the looseness of Durkheim's theoretical structure and further decreases the level of generality of his explanations.

The unsatisfactory status of psychological variables in Durkheim's theory. As we have seen, one of Durkheim's objectives was to create a *sociological* theory, dealing with social facts (such as aggregated sui-cide rates) that are to be explained by reference to other social facts (such as various states of social integration or cohesion). He main-

---

[17] For a discussion of the desideratum that a theory should be able to be proved wrong, see earlier, under "A Simple Model of Political Behavior."

42

tained that he was not concerned with variables other than social ones; in particular he eschewed an interest in psychological causes. He did acknowledge that there are individual determinants of suicide but that they are not important enough to influence the social suicide rate. "They may perhaps cause this or that separate individual to kill himself, but not give society as a whole a greater or lesser tendency to suicide." Since these psychological factors "have no social repercussions," he argued further, "they concern the psychologist, not the sociologist" [p. 51]. Here Durkheim was arguing that psychological causes should be treated as variables that are *separate* in their operation from social causes and that they are sufficiently unimportant that they may be ignored.

As we have seen, however, Durkheim also spoke of the "collective mark" that egoism, altruism, and anomie stamp on individuals and of a definite "personality type" associated with each social type of suicide. In this formulation he was treating the individual as a kind of vessel through which suicidogenic social forces flow. This formulation definitely rests on psychological generalizations, for example, that the social condition of anomie creates feelings of disorientation, irritation, and disgust and that these feelings are especially conducive to self-destruction. In this case psychological processes are treated as factors that *intervene* between the social facts (integration) and behavioral outcomes (suicide).

At this point, however, a disquieting series of questions arise. If the individual is to be treated as the vessel through which social forces flow, why don't *all* Protestants commit suicide, if they are affected by the condition of egoism generated by Protestantism? And why do *any* Catholics or Jews commit suicide? Or, alternatively, how do we account for those Protestants who do *not* commit suicide? One sympathetic to Durkheim would respond by asserting that other social forces—for example, the character of his family situation or the presence or absence of anomic conditions in his life—would augment or inhibit the religious influences. There is some merit in this response, but we should also ask whether there are not also independent psychological factors that interact with these social factors to influence not only individual suicides but also social suicide rates.

I have in mind two possible kinds of psychological factors: variables complementary to the social and variables independent of the social. It might well be, for example, that exposure to Protestantism generates an excessively strong conscience and a corresponding {21} tendency to express aggression in an inward rather than an outward direction. But this does not tell the whole story of suicide. Individuals are also equipped with a vast array of defense mechanisms and coping capacities, so that we would expect *on psychological grounds* that some individuals would be better able to withstand such self-destructive tendencies and to turn them into other lines of activity. In this case we would be treating various psychological variables as *complementing* the social forces in their impact on suicide and presumably contributing to a more refined causal statement based only on the social forces.

A final possibility is that psychological factors are responsible *both* for membership in certain social groups (such as the Protestant church) *and* for self-destructive tendencies. According to psycho-analytic explanations of suicide associated with the names of Sigmund Freud [1917, 1924] and Karl Abraham [1924], suicide is closely linked to states of personal melancholy, which is in turn based on the loss of a significant object in early periods of childhood, anger with the lost object, identification with the lost object, and the turning of the anger inward in an act that is simultaneously self-punitive and hostile. Might not this constellation of motivational forces predispose an individual to accept a religion that stresses individual conscience, self-discipline, and perhaps even masochism? If so, both commitment to a religious belief and a tendency to self-destruction would be effects of an *independent* set of psychological variables.

The upshot of these remarks is that the psychological parameters[18] in Durkheim's theory are unsatisfactory because they raise a number of unresolved issues and involve him in a number of questionable psychological formulations. Refinement of these parameters along the lines suggested would not only make his theory more realistic psycho-logically but would also create the possibility of generating a more nearly complete explanation of both individual suicides and aggregated suicide rates.

---

[18] For a definition of parameters, and a discussion of their place in the logical structure of a theory, see earlier, under "A Simple Model of Political Behavior."

Talcott Parsons' Theory of Deviance and Social Control

Though Durkheim's analysis of suicide was tied to a quite general theory of social integration, his explanation rested at a "middle range" of generality. It was directed toward a fairly restricted range of data—suicide rates—and attempted to explain variations in these data by referring to differences in social integration and regulation.

The theoretical focus of Talcott Parsons is much more general. Working to create a "general theory of action," Parsons anticipates that his framework will form a basis for explaining *all* behavior; in fact, he has worked out theoretical statements on many analytical levels—the personality, the social, the cultural, even the biological. Even his theoretical perspective on deviance and social control—on which we shall concentrate—is pitched at an abstract level. Parsons, then, has consistently been a "general" or "grand" theorist.[19]

Transition from Durkheim to Parsons: Merton's Deviance Paradigm

In order to shift from Durkheim's to Parsons' theoretical style, I shall summarize briefly Robert Merton's paradigm on deviance. It is broader in scope than Durkheim's theory of suicide in that it attempts to account for a *variety of types* of deviance, but at the same time it is not formulated at a very abstract level, as compared to Parsons. To mention Merton makes sense for another reason as well, since Parsons argues that Merton's paradigm on deviance is consistent with—indeed, is a "special case" of—his own theory of deviance [pp. 257-258].[20] We shall not analyze Merton's paradigm in great detail, however, nor shall we subject it to the same kinds of criticisms that are leveled at our four major theorists.[21]

---

[19] For an attempt to contrast the "middle-range" and "grand" styles, compare "On Sociological Theories of the Middle Range" [Merton 1968].

[20] Unless otherwise indicated, the page references in brackets in this section refer to Parsons' *The Social System*.

[21] Formal and empirical criticisms of Merton's deviance paradigm are found in Dubin 1959, Cloward 1959, and Cohen 1965. For Merton's commentary on Dubin and Cloward, see Merton 1959.

Whereas Durkheim was interested in explaining different rates of suicide, Merton focuses on all "nonconforming rather than conforming conduct" [1968, p. 186]. Despite his broader range of data, Merton's approach is similar to Durkheim's in several respects. First, he emphasizes the social genesis of deviance in contrast to explanations grounded in biological impulses or personality disorders, although he is not as thorough as Durkheim in attempting to demolish these explanations. In any case, Merton's focus is on {22} the "normal reaction of normal people to abnormal [social] conditions." Also like Durkheim, Merton is interested in *rates* of behavior—the aggregated features of deviance—not individual cases. Finally, Merton shares Durkheim's concern with a specific kind of social determinant—lack of integration.

Merton selects *anomie* as his fundamental independent variable, but he gives a somewhat different meaning from Durkheim's to this concept. Durkheim defined anomie as a lack of regulation by the normative order. Merton defines it, however, as a disjunctive relationship between cultural goals and institutionalized norms in society. As his principal example of anomie Merton chooses the American cultural goal of monetary success and asks how well this goal can be attained within the scope of institutionalized norms for doing so—getting an education, taking risks in business, and so on. Merton's answer is that the goal is not readily attainable within accepted norms, and for that reason a variety of types of deviant behavior can be expected to develop in American society.

What are the major deviant responses? Merton classifies them in terms of whether the individual accepts or rejects the cultural goal or the institutionalized norms, or both. First, *conformity* involves accepting both society's goals and its legitimately institutionalized norms. An example is the boy who wants to get rich and works hard at it by educating himself, getting a job, and making his way up the occupational ladder. Second, *innovation* involves accepting the cultural goals but rejecting the institutionalized means of attaining them. The innovator relies on new, illegitimate means such as racketeering, vice, or perhaps white-collar crime. Third, *ritualism* rejects the cultural goals while continuing to accept, indeed to overemphasize, the institutionalized norms. A familiar type of ritualist is the bureaucrat who insists on following every rule to the letter, thus choking the system with red tape and defeating organizational aims. Fourth, *retreatism* involves rejection of both cultural goals and institutionalized means of realizing them; here Merton has in mind society's outcasts—hobos, psychotics, artists, alcoholics, and drug addicts. And finally, *rebellion* involves the rejection of both cultural goals and norms and the substitution of new goals and means in their place. The rebel develops an ideology, perhaps a revolutionary one, which creates new values and norms regarded as more legitimate than the existing ones.

Schematically, Merton's paradigm of deviant responses can be represented as follows:

	Modes of Adaptation	*Cultural Goals*	*Institutionalized Means*
I	Conformity	+	+
II	Innovation	+	—
III	Ritualism	—	+
IV	Retreatism	—	—
V	Rebellion	±	±

There is an important difference between Durkheim's and Merton's methods of classifying variables. Durkheim defined suicide in general terms at the outset of his analysis. He subdivided this dependent variable in two ways—first in terms of its social causes (egoism, altruism, and so on), and second in terms of its individual psychological manifestations (here again he characterized the psychological traits of the egoistic suicide, altruistic suicide, and so on). Merton's procedure is different. Having identified the basic cause of deviance in anomie—a discontinuity between cultural goals and institutionalized norms—he classified individual responses to anomie *in terms of their modifications of the basic independent variables (goals and norms)*. Merton in short, used the same set of concepts to classify both his independent and his dependent variables.

Merton's hypotheses about the social incidence of deviant behavior are not strictly derived from, but they are consistent with, his classification of causes and outcomes. We have already indicated his most general hypothesis: deviant behavior "may be regarded sociologically as a symptom of dissociation between culturally prescribed aspirations and socially structured avenues for realizing these aspira-tions" [1968, p. 188]. One type of such dissociation occurs in a "society in which there is an exceptionally strong emphasis upon specific goals without a corresponding emphasis upon institutional procedures." The particular form of frustration in such a society—and Merton clearly has in mind the United States, where monetary success is overvalued and the means of attaining it undervalued—is that society arouses hopes in its populace but does not provide adequate oppor-tunities to realize them.

These general propositions say little about the *differential* in-cidence of the several types of deviant behavior. To specify this, Merton suggests that people in different locations in the class structure will deviate in different ways. Leaving conformity aside, Merton argues that a great dissociation between goals and institu-tionalized procedures occurs among the lower but not the lowest members of the working classes. The goal of monetary success is remote from them, and legitimate means of attaining it are largely unavailable. Consequently, Merton argues, they are {23} the most likely types of persons to reject societal means and adopt innovations, such as crime, as a mode of deviant behavior [1968, pp. 198-199]. Ritualism, by contrast, is the mode of adaptation most common in the lower middle classes. Clerks and bookkeepers are perhaps closer to the opportunities for monetary success, but if they are to make it they have to avoid risk and stick closely to the rules [1968, pp. 204-205]. Retreatism is a manifestation of the hopelessness of the very lowest orders of society, who are so far from realizing the cultural goals that they reject both the goals themselves and the means of attaining them [1968, pp. 207-208]. Finally, though Merton did not analyze rebellion very thoroughly, he suggests that rebellion is likely to be the dominant response in a social class that is rising, but not fast enough to realize its aspirations. As these illustrations show, the variable of "degree of remoteness from cultural goals and means" is an important variable in leading Merton to generate predictions about what kinds of people will choose what kinds of deviant responses.

Merton's paradigm of deviance is very much in the Durkheimian tradition. Even though it is more comprehensive in its range of data, it is still "middle range" in that it produces a series of fairly definite hypotheses. While these hypotheses are not put to the test by Merton, he did bring them to a sufficiently specific point that investigators might be guided to concrete empirical research if they wished to test their validity.

Parsons: General Perspective

In studying Parsons, we shall focus on the same topic analyzed by Durkheim and Merton—social deviance. Given the character of Parsons' analysis, however, it is not possible to plunge directly into that topic; his analysis of deviance is so closely tied to his general theoretical formulations that we must sketch a few rudiments of "general action theory" as an introduction to his theory of deviance.

The ingredients of "action." In much of Parsons' work, the starting point for analysis is the concept of an *actor*, who is, represented as a motivated, goal- seeking individual. It is convenient to identify the actor as a person, although Parsons considers it possible to treat groups and collectivities as actors as well. Because the actor is represented as goal seeking, he seeks to establish certain relations with objects in his environment. Thus the second element in the definition of action is the *ends* toward which the actor strives.

The actor, however, does not choose his ends randomly, nor does he attain them automatically. Various other factors intervene as the actor strives to maximize his satisfaction. In the first place, action takes place in a *situation*, which is significant for the actor in two respects. First, in order to attain ends, he must have *means*, such as facilities, tools, or resources; and second, he must overcome *conditions*, or obstacles to the attainment of ends. A final element of action arises from the fact that the choice of ends, the means for attaining them, and the means for overcoming obstacles are all regulated by *normative standards*. These standards underscore the fact that all action is basically social in character. It is continuously influenced by norms that arise in the interaction among individuals.

Formally defined, then, action is "(1) Behavior [of an organism] . . . oriented toward the attainment of ends or goals or other anticipated states of affairs. (2) It takes place in situations. (3) It is normatively regulated; and (4) it involves the expenditure of energy, or effort, in 'motivation'" . . . [Parsons & Shils 1951, p. 53]. Its several ingredients are represented graphically in figure 8.

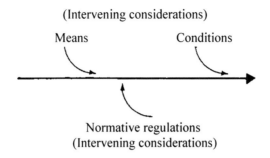

Figure 8. Elements of action [after Parsons 1937, p. 44].

There are three types of objects in the actor's environment. The first is *physical* objects, which are important to the actor as ends, means, or conditions, but with which he does not actually interact. The second is *social* objects—other actors—with which he does interact. The third is *cultural* objects—such as ideas, beliefs, and symbols—which regulate and lend meaning to action.

Systems of action. Parsons argues that all the ingredients of action have to be taken into consideration in analyzing any discrete unit act. He also argues, however, that action does not occur in isolated bits, unconnected with one another. Rather, every unit act is implicated in *systems* of action, which maintain patterns over periods of time and give structure to action. These systems of action are organized at several levels of generality. For purposes {24} of understanding his theory of deviance, the three most important systems are the personality system, the social system, and the cultural system. These three systems are linked with one another in complex relations, but we shall concentrate especially on the relations between the personality and social system.

The focus of organization of the personality system is the individual actor, and the important units of the personality are drives, attitudes, skills, conceptions of self, and so on. The academic discipline of psychology concentrates on the analysis of this system.

Social systems lie on a different level of abstraction from the personality. A social system is that set of relations arising from selected aspects of the interaction among persons. These aspects of interaction are *roles*, such as the role of husband, student, or church member. A role is only a part of a person's interaction system. For example, a student in his role as student has certain relations with instructors, deans, and other students. However, the role of student does not exhaust all the aspects of his other interactions; he is also a child to his parents, a husband to his wife if he is married, a citizen of the nation, and a resident of a locality. Nor is a role—or even all significant roles—equivalent to the personality. Personality involves the organization of action at a different analytic level. It is important to keep in mind, furthermore, that the basic units of social systems are roles, not personalities.

The central ingredient of the concept of role is the *expectation* that the actor will perform in certain ways. Roles involve normative relations; they consist of a cluster of expectations of how people should behave toward one another. Perhaps the clearest examples of expectations are found in legal codes and contracts, which spell out explicitly certain prohibitions and obligations. Criminal law explicitly prohibits physical assault; contracts stipulate when and where deliveries of goods and payments for goods are to be made. Other normative expectations—such as subtle rules of etiquette—are not so explicit, but their influence on social conduct can nevertheless be very strong.

The concept of *sanctions* refers to the means by which people attempt to secure compliance with role expectations. Sanctions, too, may be formal and explicit, such as paying a person a salary for continuing to perform his occupational role or restraining him physically if he commits a crime; but they also may be informal and subtle, such as letting a person know by a chilly silence that he is doing the wrong thing.

Having reviewed the concepts of expectation, performance, and sanction, we may now note Parsons' formal definition of a social system: "a system of interaction of a plurality of actors, in which the action is oriented by rules which are complexes of complementary expectations concerning roles and sanctions" [Parsons & Shils 1951, p. 195]. A social system is a network of interactive relationships. Furthermore, if any one of these relationships is modified or disturbed, a series of processes is set off in the system, by means of which it readjusts or undergoes certain types of change.

Figure 9 represents a simple social system, with two actors, whom Parsons labels "ego" and "alter" for convenience of reference. The social system is constituted by the interactive relationship between ego and alter. But it is also important to remember that each actor is not only involved in his relationship with the other but has his own particular situation, consisting in part of his other role involvements.

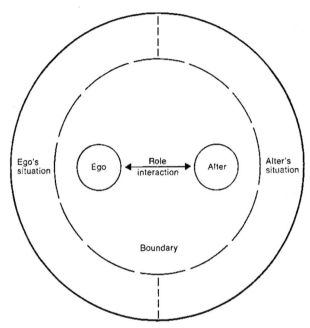

Figure 9. Simple social system.

Finally, a word should be added about cultural systems, even though they will not figure significantly in the subsequent discussion. As indicated, they are made up of ideas, values, expressive symbols, and the like; in short, a cultural system is a system of meanings. Concrete illustrations of cultural systems are a language, a religious belief system, and an organized set of mathematical relations. Cultural systems, like personality and social systems, are {25} abstractions from behavior in general and are conceived as analytically independent from other systems of action. Empirically, however, cultural systems shape behavior in the other two types of system, mainly by becoming internalized in personalities and institutionalized in social systems.

A Summary of Parsons' Theory of Deviance and Social Control

Again, our procedure will be first to give a general summary of Parsons' analysis, raising a few critical points and elaborations along the way but reserving the central theoretical criticisms until the end.

Definitions of deviance. Parsons' general definition of deviance arises from his conception of interaction, which involves two or more actors whose behavior is continuously regulated by role expectation and sanctions and continuously monitored by communication. Analytically, the starting point for defining deviance is the normative expectations that regulate behavior. If behavior is to be deviant, it has to deviate *from* some specific set of expectations. Delinquent behavior by juveniles is regarded as deviant by most members of a community but is conforming behavior from the standpoint of the norms governing the delinquent gang itself. School segregation by race is officially illegal and therefore deviant from the standpoint of the law of the land, but from the standpoint of many localities that resist integration, *de*segregation is the deviant behavior. Deviance, then, is not some intrinsic type of behavior; it is behavior assessed in relation to some normative reference point [pp. 250-251].

Formally, Parsons' definition of deviance reads as follows: "The processes by which resistances to conformity with social expectations develop, and the mechanisms by which these tendencies are or tend to be counteracted in social systems" [p. 249]. This definition, like Merton's, focuses on nonconforming behavior in general. In addition, however, Parsons' definition includes social control as an integral part of the definition, an aspect generally not considered by Merton.

Both Durkheim and Merton insisted on the distinctively social character of deviance. Parsons shares this emphasis but, in addition, considers deviance as a *relation* between individual behavior and social norms. Accordingly, we can find two additional, somewhat more specific definitions of deviance in his work, one referring to the social system, the other to the personality system. Viewed from the perspective of the social system, deviance is "the tendency on the part of one or more of the component actors to behave in such a way as to disturb the equilibrium of the interactive process" [p. 250]. According to this formulation, it is the system of interaction that is disturbed by deviant behavior. Viewed from the perspective of the person, deviance is "a motivated tendency for an actor to behave in contravention of one or more institutionalized normative patterns." While norms are mentioned in this case, the primary focus is on the actor's motivation.

The several definitions of deviance offered by Parsons may appear to contradict one another, but this is not the case. They identify different facets of the same general phenomenon, a phenomenon that is necessarily multifaceted because it has links to both the social and the personality systems. Nevertheless, if an investigator chooses one of these facets as the primary one, he predisposes himself to raise certain kinds of questions and not others. For example, Parsons chooses to emphasize two facets: the motivational orientation of the person who deviates and the system's definition of role expectations. These emphases suggest an interest in what motivates the deviant and the processes of social control that re-motivate him to return to a conforming relation with the system's norms.

Consider, however, an alternative focus. Suppose deviance is regarded in terms of neither the personality of the deviant nor the system's norms, but rather as a result of the assessment of those who have the power to wield sanctions and enforce norms as they interpret them. This definition of deviance from the perspective of the enforcer has been advanced by sociologists such as Goffman [1962] and Becker [1963]. Goffman, for example, considers that "mental illness" is not so much a matter of the motivational state of the individual "patient" as it is of certain acts of labeling people as "sick" and certain administrative decisions on the part of persons in authority—lawyers, judges, psychiatrists, and hospital officials. Such an approach raises different questions than those suggested by Parsons' definition. The motivational genesis of deviant behavior becomes relatively unimportant for a sociologist like Goffman, because the "deviant" may well be a victim of rule making and rule application by those in authority, no matter what his motivation. Parsons tends to view agents in social control more as "responding" to actions that do not conform to role expectations. Hence he is led more to ask why the expectations were violated. By the same token, Goffman is less likely to consider these aspects. This is not to say that Parsons' theory precludes analysis of the power relations between "enforcer" and "deviant," nor that Goffman's theory {26} precludes an analysis of the "deviant's" motivation. Their initial definitions, however, do not single out and highlight these respective aspects. In any case, the example should underscore the intimate link between a theorist's general perspective on a subject and the kinds of questions he may be led to pursue.

Before moving on, let us raise one set of complications regarding normative expectations, which is Parsons' reference point for defining deviance. Parsons' definition suggests that norms are relatively precise in their specification of deviant behavior (for example, "thou shalt not kill"), and as a result, behavior that is deviant in relation to these norms (killing) is readily identifiable. In examining several characteristics of social norms, however, it becomes apparent that the identification of deviant acts is sometimes a very ambiguous matter. Consider the following distinctions:

1. Explicit versus vague normative expectations. An important dimension of role expectations is the degree to which they are explicit or vague in their reference to expected performances. An explicit expectation is that a university professor is expected to meet his classes. If he does not, he is judged deviant by the university administration unless he has an acceptable excuse, such as a death in the immediate family. Another expectation is that he should publish books and articles; this expectation is somewhat vague, however, and it is difficult to determine exactly when it is being violated. If a professor publishes one article in five years, it is generally agreed that this is too little and that he has not lived up to the expectations regarding publication. On the other hand, it is sometimes asserted that a professor publishes too much, which suggests he is sacrificing quality for quantity. But there is no precise measure of pages or pounds of published materials—to say nothing of a measure of quality—to determine whether he has met the expectation adequately. This kind of loose, open expectation makes conformity and deviance difficult to identify, even though it is an extremely important expectation in determining the rewards and punishments received by an individual professor.

2. Required versus optional behavior. By and large, both meeting classes and publishing scholarly works are required features of the role of university professor. But an additional range of other behavior-attending ceremonials such as graduations, giving public speeches in the community, and the like—is frequently specified as "expected" somewhere in the university handbook. The expectation is a weak one, however, and while by strict interpretation nonperformance constitutes a case of deviance, few people become concerned about nonperformance, and no particular sanctions are applied against the

nonperformer. Thus, deviant behavior becomes more difficult to define and identify as we move from required toward optional normative expectations.

3. Required versus prohibited behavior. A third dimension of role expectations concerns whether they require or prohibit the performance of an act. Most criminal laws enjoin us not to do something; they are prohibitive. Some criminal laws, however, call for positive actions. The legal codes of some states specify a crime known as misprision of felony; these laws state that if an individual knows a felony is going to occur, he is in criminal violation if he does not report this to the authorities. Yet such a law is seldom enforced, and failure to comply is often more difficult to specify than actions that are in defiance of prohibitive laws.

Parsons' definition of deviance seem to apply most readily to certain types of norms: those that specify explicit and required performances and prohibitions, instances of which are identifiable. But such norms constitute only part of the normative order, and we would expect a different set of processes of deviance and social control to operate in the gray, borderline areas of vague and optional norms. For example, when norms are vague and optional, we would not expect processes involving simple "deviance" and "social control" so much as we would expect processes of argument and negotiation between parties as to what the norms really are and whether in fact deviance is occurring at all. These areas of ambiguity and flexibility in the social world make the phenomenon of deviance ever more relative and contingent than Parsons' definition suggests.

The organization of central concepts. Parsons' presentation of his theory of deviance is extraordinarily complex. He moves rapidly from extremely abstract concepts to very detailed empirical illustrations. He brings many variables to bear in his discussion of deviance, but he does not always place these variables in specific logical relationship to one another. Giving Parsons a sympathetic reading and at the risk of possibly oversimplifying and distorting his theory, I shall extract what appear to be the central theoretical variables, break them down into component parts, and make explicit the implicit logical relations among the variables. In short, my summary aims to recapitulate and perhaps to make more systematic the theory of deviance.

There appear to be four main types of variables in Parsons' theory: (1) Strain, which is the major factor {27} in the genesis of deviant behavior. (2) The directions of deviant behavior. Analysis of these directions provides a typology of deviant tendencies. (3) The ways in which deviant tendencies become structured. Here the question of the opportunities for deviant behavior arises. (4) Social control, or the countertendencies to deviance that arise in reaction to it. We shall consider these variables in the order listed.

1. Strain. Parsons' analytic starting point is the interactive system, which is characterized by the presence of role expectations, the mutual interplay of sanctions, and above all, the anticipation that the behavior and attitudes of each actor will conform with the expectations of the other.

The stage for the development of deviant behavior is set when, "from whatever source, a disturbance is introduced into the system [of interaction], of such character that what alter does leads to a frustration, in some important respects, of ego's expectation-system vis-à-vis alter's" [p. 252]. This disturbance constitutes "strain," because there has been a breakdown in the relationship between expectation and behavior. The concept of strain is not identical to the concept of deviance; it constitutes one of the main conditions giving rise to deviant responses. The distinction between the two may be confusing, because on some occasions deviance in one part of a social system may create strain elsewhere in the system, but still it is necessary to keep the two concepts of strain and deviance analytically separate.

As the phrase "from whatever source" indicates, Parsons is not initially concerned with the origin of disequilibrium, or strain, which initially upsets the system of interaction. It may come from any concrete source—an earthquake, the death of a leader, or the imperfect socialization of an individual into a role. The main idea is that strain on the system of interaction creates a frustration of expectations.

Although Parsons' theory is thus "open" with respect to the sources of strain, he does identify several sources in his discussion. One source of strain lies in the *specific pattern of role expectations themselves*; "the ways in which 'pressure' is exerted on the motivational system of the actor will vary as a function of the kind of pattern with which he is expected to conform" [p. 267]. For example, Parsons argues that the institutionalization of roles that are dominated by a high degree of specialization, impersonality, and expectations of achievement are likely to frustrate the immediate gratification of impulses and, consequently, are more likely to create strain than other types of social roles. By way of illustration, Parsons argues that the expectations governing the occupational roles for American adult males frustrate dependency needs, because these cannot normally be gratified in most occupational roles. Indeed, "this seems to be one of the focal points of strain in American society" [p. 269]. The institutionalization of certain types of role requirements, then, creates a predisposition toward strain in the system.

Another kind of strain arises from *role ambiguities,* in which the expectations for roles are not clear. In this connection Parsons employs a distinction noted earlier, the distinction between explicit and vague role expectations. In some roles it is difficult to know what constitutes conformity; once again, in the achievement-oriented system of American occupational roles, it is difficult to know when a person is finally to be judged a "success."

A third source of strain is *role conflict,* by which is meant "the exposure of the actors to conflicting sets of legitimized role expectations such that complete fulfillment of both is realistically impossible" [p. 280]. For example, a husband is subject to role conflict if his wife expects him to act like a man and exercise initiative, while his mother expects him to act as an obedient son. Or, a student may be subject to conflict between his anticipated future role as a scholar, which requires hard study, and his role as a member of a peer group, which requires that one not be a "grind."

Strain, then, some sources of which we have just mentioned, is one of the necessary conditions for deviant behavior. However, Parsons qualifies this causal relation in two ways: by specifying several ways to reduce strain, thereby "heading off" tendencies of deviant behavior; and by indicating several responses to strain other than deviance.

A common way of minimizing potential strain is to give greater weight to one role expectation than to another. In our society, for example, the demands of occupation and family are quite important, and often supersede other role obligations. Thus, upon receiving a dinner invitation from the wife of a friend, a housewife might say, "We'd love to accept but my children are ill and I wouldn't want to leave them with a babysitter," or "We'd love to come, but my husband has to attend a special meeting at the office." In such a case, a hierarchy is invoked to resolve any potential role conflict and minimize any strain that might arise.

Another way is to schedule potentially conflicting role performances at different times. A straightforward example is segregation of the role obligations of the job from the role obligations of the home by institutionalizing a nine-to-five job. In this way types {28} of behavior that might be appropriate to the family setting but inappropriate to the job setting, and vice versa, are structurally segregated from one another.

A third mechanism for reducing role conflict is to conceal the activities associated with one role from those associated with another. Thus, our student who both is ambitious and desires popularity studies in secret, away from his peers. To mention another example, adolescent peer groups are typically eager to keep their activities separate from parental surveillance, thus avoiding the role conflicts that would arise if both peers and parents were present.

A final mechanism for reducing role conflict is to develop certain rationalizations, whereby a set of role expectations is believed to hold in one context but not in another. A person might argue that it is acceptable for blacks to work in the same shop or belong to the same labor union as whites but not to live in a white neighborhood. Many potential rationalizations are found in a culture's proverbs, many of which contradict one another but which are uttered on separate occasions as if they held for all occasions. For example, the proverb "he who hesitates is lost," seems to be difficult to reconcile with the proverb "look before you leap." Yet each enjoys a kind of separate and absolute existence, and each is singled out to justify behavior in a situation that might involve some role conflict. Again, the cliché "business is business" is a way of saying that an actor is engaging in some behavior that might be deviant from one perspective but that the business role is such that this behavior ought not to be considered so.

Parsons also mentions a number of alternative responses to strain other than deviance. For example, a person subject to role conflict may simply withdraw from one role. Our ambitious student may decide to ignore the social pressures exerted by his peers and thus avoid role conflict. He is not exactly engaging in deviant behavior but withdrawing from the interactive system that would pose conflict for him. Or he may decide that certain gratifications are not important for him or seek to gratify his needs in other (nondeviant) ways that are not so conflict producing.

Thus strain is not a single variable but a system of variables—conditions that give rise to strain, strain itself, and mechanisms to reduce strain. Furthermore, strain gives rise to a number of responses, only one of which is deviant behavior. The concept of strain contains a miniature model of tendencies and countertendencies to strain, even though Parsons develops this model only embryonically. Further refinement of the model would require a systematic classification of the types of sources of strain, the means of reducing strain, and the alternate responses to strain and an indication of the conditions under which strain would give rise to deviance and not some other kind of response.

2. Directions of deviance. Let us suppose that the level of strain in an interactive situation is relatively high and that it is not contained or drained off in responses other than deviant behavior. We may now analyze the ways in which strain develops into deviance and the directions that deviant behavior takes.

The psychological responses to strain are complicated, involving a combination of anxiety, hostility, and fantasy. But the response most consistently emphasized by Parsons is *ambivalence.* Under conditions of strain an actor does not simply become hostile, but he responds with mixed positive and negative affects toward alter, who, after all, has been the object of gratification in the interactive system. Thus, the response to a situation of strain calls forth both a tendency for continuing conformity as well as a tendency for alienation.

In this concept of ambivalence Parsons finds his first dimension for analyzing the directions of deviance. If the alienative side of the ambivalence is dominant, the response is *compulsive alienation*; if the conformative aspect of the ambivalent response is dominant, the response is *compulsive conformity.* These two distinctions are similar to Merton's concepts of rejection and acceptance.

A second dimension for classifying the directions of deviant response is the differentiation between activity and passivity, which, Parsons notes, is "of generally recognized psychological significance" [pp. 256-257]. This is the issue in "fight versus flight," or whether the individual will attack or withdraw in the interactive situation.

Combining these two dimensions, we produce four types of deviant response, shown in figure 10. Parsons comments on the similarity of his classification scheme to Merton's four types of deviance. Com-

	Activity	Passivity
Conformative Dominance	Compulsive performance orientation	Compulsive acquiescence in status expectations
Alienative Dominance	Rebelliousness	Withdrawal

Figure 10. Four directions of deviant response [from Parsons 1951, p. 257].

pulsive performance corresponds to "innovation," compulsive {29} acquiescence to "ritualism," withdrawal to "retreatism," and rebelliousness to "rebellion" [p. 258].

Parsons adds yet another dimension to his classification. The social system is constituted of a number of actors, interacting according to a series of normative role expectations. The deviant response of an actor, whether conformative or alienative, whether active or passive, may focus on either other *actors* (social objects) or on *norms*. Subdividing each of the four deviant responses according to this distinction, we produce eight separate directions of deviant behavior, shown in figure 11.

	Compulsive Performance Orientation (Activity)		Compulsive Acquiescence Orientation (Passivity)	
	Focus on Social Objects	Focus on Norms	Focus on Social Objects	Focus on Norms
Conformative Dominance	1. Dominance	2. Compulsive enforcement	3. Submission	4. Perfectionist observance
	Rebelliousness		Withdrawal	
Alienative Dominance	5. Aggressiveness toward social objects	6. Incorrigibility	7. Compulsive independence	8. Evasion

Figure 11. Eight directions of deviant behavior [from Parsons 1951, p. 259].

To illustrate each of the eight types, the compulsively active conformist with the emphasis on social objects is the "bossy" character who pushes others around. The compulsively active conformist with emphasis on norms is the rigid enforcer of rules, the taskmaster, who goes by the book. The compulsively passive conformist who focuses on social objects is the meek type who puts himself in the position of continuously submitting to others. The compulsively passive conformist who focuses on norms also lives by the book, but instead of demanding exacting performance from others, falls into the role of the functionary who lives by the letter of the rules. The compulsively active alienated who focuses on social objects moves through the world with a chip on his shoulder, always trying to pick a fight, whatever the cause. The compulsively active alienated who focuses on norms is the person who would break rules for the sake of breaking rules, perhaps a "rebel without a cause." For him the very presence of a rule excites the impulse to flaunt it. The compulsively passive alienated who focuses on social objects becomes independent; he distrusts others, but he prefers to go his own way rather than pick a fight. And finally, the compulsively passive alienated who focuses on norms does not flaunt the rules but breaks them through various strategies of evasion.

3. The empirical structuring of deviant behavior. Figure 11 is an analytic classification of tendencies toward deviant behavior. Parsons is careful to distinguish between these analytically "pure" tendencies and the concrete ways in which these tendencies become "structured" in patterns of behavior [p. 283]. Structuring involves actual behavior of persons and groups in situations. Parsons speaks of three distinct levels of structuring of deviant tendencies—one individual and two collective. The first level of collective structuring occurs when deviants join in some sort of collectivity; the second level of collective structuring involves a threat to the legitimacy of the normative regulations themselves and an effort to replace them.[22] Let us illustrate each level:

(a) Individual deviance. Parsons speaks of the actively alienated person's predisposition toward individualized crime, and the passively alienated person's predisposition toward hoboism, bohemianism, and

---

[22] This second level of collective structuring is similar to Merton's concept of rebellion.

schizophrenia. Illness, in general, is a passive and alienative response, but Parsons points out that the person who defines himself as ill does set himself off from the social structure, but also asks to be taken care of and made well, thereby being drawn back into social interaction.

As for the compulsively active conformist, Parsons finds it difficult to find concrete examples of deviant behavior, but he does single out the "compulsive achiever who places excessive demands on himself and on others, and who may also show his alienative motives by excessive competitiveness, and incapacity to tolerate normal challenges to his security and adequacy" [p. 286]. Finally, the passive conformist is the perfectionist who evades fulfillment of expectations by never "sticking his neck out."

(b) The collectivization of deviance. Parsons next takes up the "possibility that ego can team up with one or more alters" in deviant behavior [p. 286]. By introducing this possibility, Parsons opens the topic of the "opportunity" for deviance. He considers that the presence of like-minded deviant personalities provides an additional incentive or opportunity for acting on deviant tendencies. What does the deviant gain by joining others? First, there is an increase in numbers and ability to resist sanctions. Organized crime is more effective in evading and corrupting the law than the criminal who goes it alone. Second, the deviant is more comfortable in his own alienation if he can have it approved and reinforced by others who feel the same way.

Third, and perhaps most important, the collectivization {30} of deviant tendencies allows for the emergence of the initially *ambivalent* quality of deviant behavior. By joining a collectivity of deviants, the deviant is "enabled to act out *both* the conformative and the alienative components of his ambivalent motivational structure" [p. 286]. He can gratify his alienative tendencies by defying authority and simultaneously gratify his conformative tendencies by subordinating himself to the norms of the deviant collectivity. Familiar examples of this are "honor among thieves," the notable conformity to styles and symbols within bohemian groups, and the strict discipline among alienated political groups, often matched only by their alienation from the dominant political system. In many respects, then, the collectivization of deviant behavior is a way of having one's cake and eating it.[23]

Parsons also treats certain types of group prejudice as a way of coming to terms with ambivalence. The anti-Semite, for example, holds that he, the conformist, is respectful of the ethics of fairness and honesty in the occupational world but that the Jew is the shrewd, sneaky, unfairly competitive deviant. In this case the psychological mechanism of projection plays an important role in splitting the ambivalence. The anti-Semite projects the alienative side of his ambivalence outside, while retaining the conformative side for himself. For this reason, prejudice is characteristically accompanied by feelings of moral righteousness.

(c) The collectivization of deviance that challenges legitimacy. This type of deviance involves not only breaking existing norms but challenging the system as a whole, and perhaps substituting new norms and values. It, too, is characterized by ambivalence. Many revolutionary movements attempt to legitimize themselves by pointing out that they are the "true" representatives of the fundamental value system of the society in question, thus adopting a position of wishing to destroy the system (alienative), but in the name of the system's own values (conformative). Members of revolutionary movements may also be ambivalent toward the norms of the society they are attacking. Parsons gives the following example:

> The Communists certainly often quite self-consciously exploit the patterns of freedom of speech and the like in liberal societies, but certainly in the rank and file there is widespread feeling that in justice they have a right to expect every "consideration" from the law. But, at the same time that they insist on this right they indulge in wholesale denunciation of the "system" of which it is an institutionalized part . . . it scarcely seems possible, considering the processes of recruitment of the position of such a movement in our society, that very many of its

---

[23] Without denying the importance of this insight, I should like to suggest that the structuring of individual forms of deviance also gratifies both sides of the ambivalence. Parsons himself mentions the hospital patient who, by virtue of being ill, passively withdraws from the scene; but at the same time, by being a "good patient" living up to all hospital regulations, he is simultaneously a ritualist, a passive conformer as well as a passive withdrawer.

members should be anything but deeply ambivalent about the position they have taken [pp. 294-295].

4. Social control. Thus far we have been dealing only with the tendencies toward deviance in an interactive system. The final major variable in Parsons' theory is social control or "the forestalling of . . . deviant tendencies . . . and the processes by which, once under way, these [tendencies] can be counteracted and the system brought back in the relevant respects to the old equilibrium state" [p. 298].

In the passage just quoted, Parsons distinguishes between the prevention of deviance—"forestalling"—on the one hand, and the containment and control of deviance on the other. The line between these two types of control is not always easy to draw, but the distinction provides a convenient basis for discussing the arguments developed by Parsons.

With respect to the prevention of deviance, we have already mentioned a number of ways of "easing" frustrating situations, especially role conflict-hierarchical priorities among roles, time scheduling of activities, concealment, and rationalization. By reducing strain these strategies lessen the probability of deviant behavior and may therefore be considered as a very general type of control over deviant behavior. In addition, Parsons identifies a number of institutionalized possibilities for "acting out" deviant tendencies in legitimate or quasi-legitimate settings, so that these tendencies are not "dammed up," only to emerge as deviant behavior elsewhere. Parsons provides two examples: *(a)* the ritualized expression of tension at times of great stress, such as the funeral ritual, which is supported socially and which "serves to organize the reaction system in a positive manner and to put a check on the disruptive tendencies" [p. 304]. *(b)* various "secondary institutions," such as "youth culture," which are relatively permissive. Youth culture may be regarded as a "safety valve" that allows people to "raise hell" in a tension-generating period of life. Activities such as reunions, celebrations, and athletic events often serve the same function. Parsons treats secondary institutions mainly as drain-off mechanisms to control deviant behavior, {31} but he also notes that they border on deviance themselves and may pass over the line. Gambling, for example, is a control in the sense that it "relieves the strains by permitting a good deal of [deviant] behavior, and yet keeping it sufficiently within bounds so that it is not too disruptive in the opposite direction" [p. 307]. Carried to excess, however, gambling comes to be treated as a case of full-fledged deviance.

With respect to the *containment* and *control* of deviance Parsons also mentions several different mechanisms. We shall consider isolation, insulation, and the paradigm of social control processes, the last of which restores rather than merely contains deviant tendencies.

The prototypical case of isolation is the incarceration of the criminal who, in the extreme case, is simply kept apart from others, and no effort is made to rehabilitate or restore him to social functioning. A similar case would be the removal of the mentally ill to "insane asylums" in order to put them out of the way. In recent times, the relations between isolation and rehabilitation has become blurred, as some reforms have led to treating the criminal and the insane as "sick" and "possibly to be helped" as well as "dangerous."

The line between isolation and insulation is not always clear. In general, however, insulation does not involve such deliberate "structuring out" of the deviant from the system, is not so complete in its prevention of interaction between deviant and dominant culture, and allows for the voluntary return of the deviant from the insulated sector of the larger society. An example of insulation would be placing the ill into hospitals for a temporary stay. The self-imposed insulation of deviant subgroups in geographical areas such as Greenwich Village and the Left Bank of Paris may also serve the function of minimizing day-by-day contact between the deviant group and the larger society. Of course, publicizing these groups in the mass media tends to counteract these insulative mechanisms and partially reintroduces the groups back into the social order.

Finally, Parsons outlines a paradigm of social control processes. These may be combined with other mechanisms such as insulation, but they also involve a more or less deliberate effort to facilitate the return of the deviant to acceptable behavior as defined by the dominant culture. This paradigm of social control could be illustrated in many settings—the religious confessional, criminal rehabilitation, Alcoholics Anonymous, and the like—but I shall use Parsons' most developed example, psychotherapy, as a form of restorative social control.

Parsons considers that mental illness is *motivated* deviance. In this assertion he is squarely in line with psychoanalytic tradition, which treats mental illness as rooted in neurotic conflict and other motivational features of the individual. Parsons suggests that psychotherapeutic settings involve a number of processes that increase the probability that the patient will be motivated to return to conformity with various role expectations—particularly familial and occupational ones—from which his illness had permitted him to withdraw.

The first ingredient of psychotherapy is *generalized support* that is given to the person who is ill. He is not simply rejected. In the psychotherapeutic relationship the establishment of basic trust between the therapist and the patient is essential to the relearning of various types of motivation, commitments, and role expectations. This support reincorporates the mentally disturbed person into a meaningful social relationship and reduces the chances that he will withdraw from interaction altogether.

The second condition is *permissiveness*. In the psychotherapeutic setting the patient is permitted to bring to the surface various deviant tendencies, but the psychotherapist typically does not take a moralistic or blaming attitude toward the patient. Such a stance permits the patient to gain a new level of understanding of the deviant behavior.

A third condition, closely related to permissiveness, is that the therapist *refuses to reciprocate* or gratify the patient's demands. If the patient expresses anger, the therapist does not fight back; if the patient is seductive, the therapist does not join him in collectively acting out the deviant tendencies. This frustration of deviant tendencies is an important ingredient of the situation in which motivational re-learning can take place.

Finally, the psychotherapist is in the position to *manipulate rewards.* He is able to reward insights and corrective emotional relearning on the part of the patient and thus "to bring him back," as it were, to greater mental health and to restore his ability to conform to role expectations. Such, in capsule, is Parsons' theory of restorative social control as illustrated by psychotherapy.

Thus the social system is equipped with a variety of controls— drain-off mechanisms, buffers, isolation, insulation, and social structures specializing in restorative social control—all of which are counterdeterminants to deviant tendencies. Parsons treats these as ways of restoring the social system to the kind of equilibrium state that existed prior to the introduction of disturbance and strain into the system. {31} It should be clear, however, that this model of restorative equilibrium is presented by Parsons as an analytic model, not as an unqualified empirical generalization. He does not maintain that deviant tendencies always are or should be controlled and the social system thereby returned to normal functioning. In fact, he links his analysis of deviance with his theory of social change—developed elsewhere in his writings—with the following concluding sentence in his chapter on deviance: "Structured deviant behavior tendencies, which are not successfully coped with by the control mechanisms of the social system, constitute one of the principal sources of change in the structure in the social system" [p. 321].

Summary. We have reviewed four major classes of variables in the development of Parsons' theory of deviance—the genesis of strain, the directions and types of deviance itself, the structuring of deviance, and social control. The review has indicated at least an implicit logical ordering among the four classes of variables. Each can be considered as logically prior to the other. Strain, for example, is a necessary condition for the development of a deviant tendency. A deviant tendency is a necessary condition for the empirical structuring of deviance. And finally, the presence of some sort of deviant behavior is a necessary condition for the activation of processes of social control. Parsons himself does not make these priorities explicit, but his discussion reveals this cumulative sequence of variables that constitute the model of deviance and control.

Some Criticisms Regarding the Logic and Testability of Parsons' Theory

A specific criticism: the correspondence with Merton's paradigm. Earlier we noted Parsons' claim that fourfold classification of deviance constituted a generalization of Merton's paradigm or, to put it in another way, that Merton's paradigm "is a very important special case" of his classification. According to Parsons, the correspondences are as follows:

Parsons	*Merton*
"Equilibrated condition of the interactive system" [p. 258]	Conformity
Compulsive performance (active conformity)	Innovation
Compulsive acquiescence (passive conformity)	Ritualism
Rebelliousness (active alienation)	Rebellion
Withdrawal (passive alienation)	Retreatism

The cases of equilibrated condition and conformity, compulsive acquiescence and ritualism, and withdrawal and retreatism appear to be relatively straightforward instances of logical parallelism, and justify Parsons' claim. The cases of compulsive performance and innovation, as well as rebelliousness and rebellion, are more questionable. It will be recalled that Merton cites several types of criminal activity as the main examples of innovation. Immediately a question arises: is it appropriate to consider crime an instance of "active conformity"? If we follow the logical parallel proposed by Parsons, it should be considered so. Subsequently, however, Parsons himself observes that it is the "actively *alienated* [that is, rebellious] person [who] is predisposed toward individualized crime." [p. 284, emphasis added.] Whether directly or indirectly, Parsons thus assigns criminal activity to both the conformative and the alienative mode. With respect to the parallel between rebelliousness and rebellion, Parsons considers rebelliousness to be a case of active alienation, whereas Merton considers it to be alienation from goals and means, *plus* a substitution of and attraction to a new system of goals and means. These kinds of asymmetries between Parsons' and Merton's classificatory schemes suggest that Parsons' claim of the "special case" is overextended and that the two schemes should more appropriately be regarded as similar in some but not all respects.

A more general criticism: the problem of derivation. One of the statements made by Parsons about the classification of directions of deviance concerns "its direct derivation from the analysis of the interaction paradigm [p. 257]. The precise reference of the phrase "the interaction paradigm" is not entirely clear in this passage, but we may assume that it involves the main components of action (actors, means, condition, ends, norms), as well as the fundamentals of inter-action (ego, alter, expectations, roles, sanctions). A classification of deviance derived from this paradigm would presumably involve the same concepts that denote the interaction paradigm itself—over-conformity with expectations, underconformity with expectations, oversanctioning, undersanctioning, overemphasis on ends, overem-phasis on means, and so on.[24] {33}

In what sense does Parsons "derive" the categories of compulsive performance, compulsive acquiescence, rebelliousness, and with-drawal from the interaction paradigm? The first dimension on which the classification is built is ambivalence, which is not derived from the categories of the interaction paradigm itself but is posited as a typical response when an ego's relations with alter are disturbed or frustrated under conditions of strain. But hostility—and the resulting ambi-valence—is not a consequence that follows necessarily from the categories of the interaction paradigm, nor is it the only empirical consequence of strain on the interaction system.[25] We might ask, then, why only one of several possible, nonderived psychological reactions to strain on the interaction system was chosen as a primary dimension for the classification of directions of deviance.

The second dimension on which the classification is built is *activity-passivity*, another dimension relating to the actor's orienta-tion to action. Parsons argues that this is "a direct derivative of the fundamental paradigm of interaction itself." He considers it as "one primary aspect of the mutual orientation of ego and alter to each other as objects" [p. 257n]. Activity is a derivation whereby an actor takes "a larger degree of control over the interaction process, than the role-expectations call for"; passivity is the opposite. Once again, while such a distinction is perfectly consistent with the interaction para-

---

[24] In this sense Merton's classification of deviance is more nearly "derived" in that the basic types of deviance are describable in precisely the same terms as his basic categories of social analysis—cultural goals and institutional means. It should be noted, however, that "rebellion" in Merton's scheme constitutes an atypical case, because in this case he permits the introduction of the "±" with respect to both ends and means but does not consider any of the other possibilities raised by this double notation [see Dubin 1959, pp. 147-150].

[25] Parsons notes that "another very important phenomenon of reaction to strain is the production of phantasies" [p. 253n]. Anxiety is also mentioned as a typical response, as well as defensive-adjustment mechanisms [p. 485].

digm, it is not developed elsewhere as a fundamental or logically necessary feature of the paradigm; furthermore, the sense in which it is logically derived from the interaction paradigm is not clear. Parsons' "derivations" leave unanswered the question as to why these two types of individual reactions to institutionalized role expectations, rather than others, were chosen as the basis for theoretical classification of deviant tendencies.

The most general criticism: the incompleteness of the theory of deviance and social control. In our summary of Parsons' theory of deviance and control, we attempted to make explicit the logical ordering among the major variables that constitute the theory—strain, directions of deviance, the empirical structuring of deviance, and social control. Considering the variables in the order listed, each prior variable may be conceived as a necessary condition for the following one, with the outcome—social deviance—being a product of the cumulation and interaction among the several variables.

This implied logical ordering, however, is very loose. With respect to strain, Parsons lists a variety of sources, each of which may give rise to strain or a number of other responses. Strain, in turn, is a necessary condition for the development of deviant tendencies, but it is not a sufficient condition; other responses are envisioned, but the conditions under which they, rather than deviant tendencies, will occur are not specified. Furthermore, the various tendencies to deviance may become structured empirically in a variety of ways. Finally, once deviance has arisen, it may be completely controlled or partially controlled, or it may spill over into processes of change in the social system. In these ways Parsons' theory of deviance is characterized by a kind of openness or indeterminacy with respect to specific outcomes.

Parsons' theory thus contrasts with Durkheim's theory of suicide in that it is less able to produce precise propositions. Durkheim attempted to associate *specific* kinds of integration and regulation with suicide rates in *specific* social groups. While his classification of different types of social integration and regulation posed serious ambiguities, his propositions were relatively precise and lent themselves in principle to direct empirical confirmation or disconfirmation.[26] By contrast, the type of propositions emerging from Parsons' analysis is that a *general class* of independent variables (for example, the several types of strain) are causally linked to a *general class* of dependent variables (for example, the several directions of deviance). Because of this looseness of theoretical structure, it is not possible to relate a specific type of strain (for example, role conflict) to a specific deviant tendency (for example, compulsive conformity). For the same reason, the "propositions" or "laws" in Parsons' theory take on a correspondingly indeterminate form. Consider, for example, Parsons' citation of a "law of motivational process":

> Strain, defined as some combination of one or more of the factors of withdrawal of support, interference with permissiveness, contravention of internalized norms and refusal of approval for value performance, results in such reactions as anxiety, fantasy, hostile impulses, and resort to the defensive-adjustment mechanism . . . [p. 485].

The indefiniteness of this "law" arises from the fact {34} that there are many classes of variables on both the independent and the dependent variable side, and the relations among these variables on each side are among the several variables.

Arising from this theoretical incompleteness is a corresponding methodological and empirical incompleteness. Because Parsons' theory of deviance and social control is indeterminate and because it does not produce specific, hypotheses, a detailed methodology or research design by which it might be tested cannot be proposed. For example, because strain is not a sufficient condition for deviance, strain may exist without producing deviant behavior; for this reason, it is not possible to know what strength of empirical association between "strain" and "deviance" is required to be significant. Furthermore, while Parsons does illustrate the various categories in his theory empirically—withdrawal by hoboism and schizophrenia, for example, and the process of social control by the therapeutic process—it is impossible to ascertain what kinds of data would be required to confirm the theory, because the theory's propositions are not definite enough to call for specific relations among empirical indicators.

---

[26] In practice, however, Durkheim relied on a number of residual categories to reinterpret and accommodate apparently disconfirmatory results.

Parsons' theory, then, appears to be less complete than Durkheim's with respect to facing the main criteria of theoretical adequacy. Although Parsons' theory is a comprehensive set of classifications and partial empirical connections, it fails to specify the conditions under which empirical associations should be expected and it does not specify canons for testing such relationships. While Durkheim's empirical methodology left much to be desired, while his results are far from convincing, and while his interpretations of data are vulnerable, he was nevertheless able to bring his theoretically related propositions to a level of specificity that allowed him to conduct primitive empirical tests and permitted the critic to assess these tests. Parsons' theory falls short of this specificity and therefore does not permit such detailed criticism. For this reason we have pitched our main criticisms at a more general level, corresponding to the more general level of his formulations.

These observations suggest that Parsons' theory stands most in need of greater specification—of the conditions under which strain leads to deviance, the conditions under which one type of deviance tends to excite one type of social control, the conditions under which social control tends to be effective or ineffective. Such specification would give his paradigm greater theoretical adequacy and bring it closer to direct testability.

Karl Marx's Theory of Economic Organization and Class Conflict

In considering the work of Karl Marx, we move back in time forty years before Durkheim wrote *Suicide* and almost eighty-five years before Parsons developed his theory on deviance. Marx's work, moreover, contrasts sharply with that of Durkheim and Parsons in several substantive respects. First, that part of Marxist theory we have chosen deals with large-scale societal forces, as well as the evolution of societies from one form to another; the focus of Parsons and Durkheim was more on the relations between the individual and his social environment and the kinds of individual behavior that were produced by this relationship. (We should not push this contrast too far, however. Durkheim also had a vision of long-term historical evolution [Bellah 1959], and elsewhere in Parsons' work we find analyses of the systematic qualities of entire societies, as well as their evolution over the centuries [Parsons 1966].) Second, both Durkheim and Parsons took social integration as their starting point and treated their respective dependent variables—suicide and deviant behavior—as manifestations of the failure of integration. Moreover, in the segments of Durkheim's and Parsons' theories we considered, individual and group conflict arises as a by-product of the failures in the integration of a system. By contrast, Marx regarded social conflict as a necessary and endemic feature of all known societies in human history. While the integration and conflict perspectives may well be reconcilable in principle,[27] integration occupies a more central place in the work of Durkheim and Parsons, whereas conflict holds a more central place in the work of Marx. Third, the authors differ in their treatment of values and ideas as determinants of social action. Durkheim stressed the importance of moral principles as integrative forces, and Parsons identifies normative expectations as important determinants of social action. Marx conceived of values, norms, and ideas primarily as by-products of more fundamental economic and social forces. His position is summarized in the following well-known statement:

> In the social production which men carry on, they enter into definite relations that are indispensible and in-dependent of their will; these relations of production correspond to a definite stage of development of their {35} material powers of production. The sum total of these relations of production constitutes the economic structure of society—the real foundation, on which rise legal and political superstructures and to which corres-pond definite forms of social consciousness. The mode of production in material life determines the general char-acter of the social, political, and spiritual processes of life. It is not the consciousness of men that determines their existence, but, on the contrary, their social exist-ence determines their consciousness [Marx 1859, p. 11].

Despite these differences in perspective, we shall ask the same questions of Marx as we did of Durkheim and Parsons. We shall ask how he organized his ideas and how he applied them to historical

---

[27] Lewis Coser attempted one kind of reconciliation in his *The Functions of Social Conflict*; Ralf Dahrendorf attempted another in *Class and Class Conflict in Industrial Society*.

data; on the basis of our answers, we shall attempt to assess the scientific adequacy of Marx's effort. In one respect it is difficult to approach Marx in this way. Marx led a most diversified life as a scholar, journalist, ideologue, and revolutionary. His work reflects this diversity. A book like *Capital* is a work simultaneously in economics, sociology, political science, philosophy, and explicit ideological debate. Therefore it is difficult, if not outright unfair, to attempt to select the theoretical or scientific aspect of Marx's work for special treatment.[28] It should be noted, however, that Marx himself conceived the "ultimate aim" of *Capital* to be a scientific one—"to lay bare the economic law of motion of modern society" [p. xix].[29] Furthermore, he welcomed "every opinion [of his work] based on scientific criticism" [p. xx].

Our treatment of Marx will be selective in still another sense. Only *Capital* will be considered. This means that many differences between *Capital* and his other works will be disregarded. Furthermore, we shall not consider the subsequent fate of the ideas found in *Capital*—for example, the discrediting of the labor theory of value, on which *Capital* is founded, and the various efforts of socialist scholars to reshape Marxist thought in the past century. In short, we shall be treating *Capital* as a self-contained enterprise, as Marx's most mature effort to explain the workings of the capitalist system.

A Selective Summary of Marx's Analysis

Marx's starting point: the labor theory of value. Marx began his analysis with a treatment of the concept "commodity," which he defined as an "object outside us, a thing that by its properties satisfies human wants of some sort or another" [p. 1]. As an economist he asked first what makes a commodity valuable, or wherein lies its source of value. Marx worked toward an answer to this question in an essentially analytic way, by breaking up what we usually think of as a physical commodity—a sack of sugar, a kitchen table, a car, and so on—into unfamiliar aspects for purposes of his analysis. In the first instance a commodity is valuable because it is useful in the process of

---

[28] Eric Hobshawn has indicated the kinds of distortions that might arise in attempting to analyze Marx piecemeal [1964].

[29] Unless otherwise noted, page references in this section are to Marx's *Capital*.

consumption. We eat corn, we build tools with iron, and we use automobiles to move ourselves from place to place. Marx argued that this use value of a commodity has nothing to do with how much human labor has gone into producing it. Water is very useful, indeed necessary, for human survival, but it takes little or no human labor to produce it. Furthermore, use values become real only as the commodity is actually consumed.

A second important aspect of a commodity's value is what it will bring in the market, or what it can be exchanged for. This is its exchange value. Marx noted that at first sight exchange values are very evasive, because they change continuously from time to time, from place to place, and from market to market. Nevertheless, he continued to pursue the question of why two commodities—for example, two pounds of sugar and one pound of iron—exchange for one another. Because they do exchange, he reasoned, the two commodities necessarily have something in common. What is this something? First, he indicated what this something is *not*—it is not "either a geometrical, a chemical, or any other natural property of commodities" [p. 4]. These features make up the *use* value of commodity, and these uses are qualitatively different from one another; it is thus impossible to compare or consider as equivalent the different uses of a sack of sugar and a piece of iron. Marx eliminated with this argument use value as the determinant of exchange value.[30]

If use value does not determine what a commodity will bring in the market, what does? Marx answered as follows: "if . . . we leave out of consideration the use-value of commodities, they have only one common property left, that of being products of labor" [p. 4]. The exchange values of all commodities are thereby reduced to "one and the same sort of labor, human labor in the abstract" [p. 5]. Simply stated, {36} Marx's position is that the exchange value of an object is determined by the amount of human labor that has gone into its production. Figure 12 summarizes this position:

---

[30] For other uses of the argument by elimination, see earlier, pp. 12-13, and later, pp. 53-54.

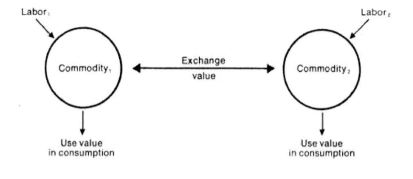

Figure 12. Labor equivalents in commodities.

Basically, then, use value and exchange value are independent. As Adam Smith's famous example shows, the exchange value of diamonds is greater than that of water, but the use value of water is greater than that of diamonds. At the same time, Marx noted some peculiarities in the relationship between the two types of value. Some commodities, such as "air, virgin soil, natural meadows, etc." [p. 7] can have use value without any exchange value. Also, some things are useful products of human labor but do not have exchange value as a commodity—for example, human labor devoted to one's own satisfaction. In order for a thing to be a commodity, it has to have *some* use value for others, or social use value. And finally, if a person puts a great deal of labor into something of no use value at all, it has no exchange value. Aside from these qualifications, however, Marx maintained that the relationship between use value and exchange value is indeterminate and that exchange value depends only on the amount of human labor incorporated into commodities.

Such, in outline, is the labor theory of value. It is the kernel of Marx's theory of capitalism. Step by systematic step he moved from this simple conception to more and more complicated formulations, bringing new considerations and assumptions to bear, until he created a model of an entire economic system. Let us now retrace his steps in that logical journey.

Extensions and qualifications on the simple labor theory of value.
The essence of the labor theory of value is contained in the following
statement: "as values, all commodities are only definite masses of
congealed labor-time" [p. 6]. Soon after formulating this principle,
Marx qualified and extended it in several ways.

Recall that Marx distinguished between a qualitative and a quantitative aspect of commodities. The qualitative aspect is found in use
values, which differ from commodity to commodity. The quantitative
aspect, or that which all commodities have in common, is found in
the exchange value. Marx made a similar distinction between the
qualitative and quantitative aspects of the labor embodied in
commodities. Labor devoted to producing particular use values is
called "useful labor." This type of labor differs from one product to
another. "As the coat and the linen are two qualitatively different use
values, so also are the two forms of labor that produce them, tailoring
and weaving" [p. 8]. Different types of useful labor are not comparable
with one another.

How, then, is labor quantitatively comparable? Marx left aside the
useful character of labor and argued that what is left is a simple
"expenditure of human labor-power," or the productive "expenditure
of human brains, nerves, and muscles" [p. 11]. This conception
assumes that work drains the potential for effort from the worker at a
certain rate. How do we measure this simple, abstract labor? Simply
by counting the amount of time spent in working. This quantitative
aspect of labor—which Marx termed "simple average labor"—is what
he used as the basis for the labor theory of value. In any concrete
situation both useful labor and simple average labor are intermingled;
Marx simply discarded the useful form analytically and retained the
simple quantity of labor, which is measured in terms of hours, days,
and weeks worked.

A problem immediately arises, however. If we rely on simple
average labor, do we measure the labor of the skilled violinmaker—
which is measured by hours to be sure—by the same units as that of
the common laborer? How do we handle the problem of divergent
skills? Marx solved this problem by a simple sort of reduction. He
argued that "skilled labor counts only as simple labor intensified, or
rather, as multiplied simple labor, a given quantity of skill being considered equal to a greater quantity of simple labor" [p. 11]. He added,
"Experience shows that this reduction is constantly being made."

The labor of the violinmaker should thus be considered as some multiple of that of the common laborer. In the last analysis, however, and "for simplicity's sake," Marx decided that "we shall henceforth account for every kind of labor to be unskilled, simple labor; by this we do no more than save ourselves {37} the trouble of making the reduction [from skilled to unskilled]" [p. 12].

Marx also noted that the value of a commodity should not be calculated by counting the number of hours taken to produce it under all conditions, but by counting the hours of what he calls *socially necessary labor time*. By this he meant that the exchange value of a commodity is determined by the amount of labor time "required to produce an article under normal conditions of production, and with the average degree of skill and intensity prevalent at the time" [p. 6]. In this way Marx introduced the level of technology as a variable to qualify the simple labor theory of value. It is not possible to apply the theory both to a piece of cloth woven by a hand loom and to another cloth woven by a machine operative. The former spends more time in producing his commodity, but its exchange value is not as great as that made by the machine operative, who spends less time. In order to apply the labor theory of value strictly, technology, or socially necessary labor, must be held constant. If labor is to be compared under different technological conditions, appropriate modifications of the measuring procedure must be made.

Marx's most important qualification of the labor theory of value is that labor power itself can be treated as a commodity that can be bought and sold. In other words, the value of labor itself is determined by the labor theory of value. Consider first an analogy. We buy a refrigerator new and lay out a certain amount of money for it. But in order to keep it running, we have to consume a certain amount of electricity, and we have to repair it now and then. All this costs time and money. The case is similar with labor power. It takes time, money, food, and effort to train the laborer in his skill. It also takes a day-to-day maintenance in the form of food, shelter, opportunities for relaxation, and so forth, to guarantee his continuous appearance in the market. To provide these things requires other people's labor. Furthermore, "[the] value of labor-power is determined, as in the case of every other commodity, by the labor time necessary for the production, and consequently also the reproduction, of this special article" [p. 149]. Thus the laborer's power, having an exchange value, can be bought and sold on the market like any other commodity. As we shall see, this formulation is central to Marx's entire theory of the creation of capital.

Marx expressed his basic labor theory of value—that the relationship among commodities is an expression of the relative amounts of abstract labor congealed in the commodities—in a variety of ways. For example, he identified the "relative form of value," in which one commodity, such as a coat, is made equal to twenty yards of linen. In stating this, we are equating "the labor embodied in the former to that in the latter" [p. 18]. He also identified the "total or expanded form of value," in which a series of commodity equivalencies are stated in relation to one another. This formulation is simply an expansion of the relative form and shows the total list of relative values of commodities, each expressing the amount of labor congealed in it. Finally, Marx stated the "general form of value," which expresses *all* the commodity values in terms of one commodity. Marx chose linen as the illustrative commodity [p. 35], but it proved a simple step to move from linen to money as the common commodity [pp. 39-41]. In these ways Marx extended the basic theory in various directions, yielding a more complete picture of possibilities and complications. But in the end, all these extensions rest on, and can be traced back to, the simple labor theory of value.

Extension of the labor theory of value to exchange. As commodities with different use values come to be produced in larger quantities, and as exchange grows and becomes a normal social act, "some portion at least of the products of labor must be produced with a special view to exchange" [p. 60]. Furthermore, as exchange increases, there arises the necessity for a more or less universal measure of value and standard of price to facilitate exchange. Such is Marx's theory of the origin of money.

The development of a money system, however, does not modify the labor theory of value, which still stands as the foundation of the economy. Early in his discussion of the exchange process, Marx reminded his readers that "every commodity is a symbol, since, in so far as it is value it is only the material envelope of the human labor spent upon it" [p. 63]. Likewise, money is also a symbol, once removed from the ultimate standard, human labor.

Marx's general formula for what happens when exchange occurs is:

Commodity——*Money*——*Commodity,*

   or

$$C——M——C$$

A weaver sells his linen for money, then purchases a Bible with the money.

> The result of the whole transaction, as regards the weaver is this, that instead of being in possession of the linen, he now has the Bible; instead of his original commodity, he now possesses another of the same value but of different utility. In like manner he procures his other means of subsistence and means of production. From his point of view, the whole process {38} effectuates nothing more than the exchange of the product of his labor for the product of someone else's, nothing more than an exchange of products [p. 78].

The prices in these transactions are nothing more than the "money-name of the labor realized in a commodity" [p. 74]. Of course, the exchange relationship and the price rest on the conception of socially necessary labor time. If weaving technology changes—for example, if a power loom is introduced to take the place of a hand loom—the exchange ratio of the prices changes accordingly. "The effect is the same as if each individual weaver had expended more labor-time upon his particular product than is socially necessary" [p. 80].

It is possible to complicate this basic formula of exchange by introducing rents and taxes and other types of payments, each of which is a special aspect of money, and each of which, by reduction, can be treated as a representation of commodities with certain values. It is even possible to generalize the formula to international exchange and to show how money develops as a complicated international standard. Any exchange system, whether simple or complex, emerges in the following form:

> The total circulation of commodities in a given country during a given period is made up on the one hand of numerous isolated and simultaneous partial metamor-

phoses, sales which are at the same time purchases, in which each coin changes its place only once, or makes only one move; on the other hand of numerous distinct series of metamorphoses, partly running side by side, and partly coalescing with each other, in each of which series each coin makes a number of moves, the number being greater or less according to circumstances [p. 95].

The nature of capital and the riddle. Up to this point we have created a picture of society with men devoting their labor to commodities—and thereby imparting value to them—and exchanging them by using coin, money, and other standards of value. This picture, however, reveals nothing about either capital or capitalism, which were the prime objects of Marx's analysis. In fact, we have not mentioned the word "capital" at all. Marx went on to derive the concept of capitalist society by introducing a series of new notions, especially that of surplus value. Let us first outline his general concept of capital.

The basic formula for the circulation of commodities is:

$$C——M——C$$

In such an exchange the individual obtains a variety of different commodities in order to use them. The weaver gives up his linen for others to use and receives his Bible and other commodities to put them to his own use. Commodities continuously drop out of circulation as they are used. Money serves as a generalized medium, a standard of price, and a measure of value and lubricates the process of exchange.

The basic formula for capital is different:

$$M——C——M$$

In this case the object is to buy a commodity in order to sell it for money; the purchaser's interest is not in the use of the commodity but in the process of exchange itself.

At first sight it appears nonsensical for an individual to purchase a commodity with money and then purchase money with that commodity. It is as if he bought linen with corn and then used the linen to buy back the same corn. Given this apparent absurdity, Marx argued that the transaction for capital was not simply $M\text{---}C\text{---}M$ but rather:

$$M\text{---}C\text{---}M'$$

with M' being *larger* than M. The capital transaction, therefore, must be devoted to the increase of money, "the increment or excess over the original value." Marx called this increment "surplus-value" [p. 128].

Marx's technical definition of surplus value, then, is buying cheaper in order to sell dearer. Furthermore, the creation of capital—or surplus value—is part of the very process of circulation. The capitalist, however, unlike the consumer, is not interested in the use value of commodities. "The restless never-ending process of profit-making alone is what he aims at" [p. 130]. The capitalist is a "rational miser," because he continuously increases his supply of money "by constantly throwing it afresh into circulation" [p. 131]. He pursues "value in process, money in process, and, as such, capital" [p. 132].

Having defined capital, Marx then presented his readers with a riddle. By his definition capital originates in the circulation of commodities. But how, he asked, can *new* value, or surplus value, be created in the process of circulation? After all, the origin of value is in labor, and the process of circulation itself involves no new labor. Marx considered a number of possible answers to this riddle, such as selling at prices deviating from their values, speculation, and so on, but he concluded that these practices could create no new value but could only redistribute existing value. After a long and somewhat tortured series of arguments, Marx concluded: "[turn] and twist then as we may, the fact remains unaltered. If {39} equivalents are exchanged, no surplus-value results, and if non-equivalents are exchanged, still no surplus-value. Circulation, or the exchange of commodities, begets no value" [p. 141]. On the verge of discovering the secret of capital, Marx apparently concluded both that it is impossible for capital to be produced in circulation and that it is equally impossible to have it originate apart from circulation. Marx's famous "double result" is that "[capital] must have its origin both in circulation and not in circulation" [p. 144]. How, then, can capital be created?

The nature of the commodity of labor. Marx did not leave his readers long to contemplate the riddle. Immediately after posing it, he revealed its answer. The capitalist is able to locate and create capital in the commodity of labor. This commodity alone possesses characteristics that permit the build-up and drain-off of surplus value and therefore for the creation of capital and a capitalist class.

Labor power, Marx argued, is a unique type of commodity. It is a "commodity, whose use-value possesses the peculiar property of being a source of value, whose actual consumption, therefore, is itself an embodiment of labor, and consequently, the creation of values" [p. 145]. As the value of labor is used or consumed, new value is created. Furthermore, labor power, like any other commodity, must be continuously renewed if it is to be used in production. Furthermore, this process of renewal can be defined in terms of the quantity of labor that is required to keep labor power producing. Marx formally defined labor power as "the aggregate of those mental and physical capabilities existing in a human being, which he exercises whenever he produces a use-value of any description" [p. 145]. The value of these capabilities, moreover, is reducible to "the labor-time necessary for the production, and consequently also the reproduction, of this special article [of labor power]" [p. 149].

How is the value of labor power measured? First, Marx argued that we would have to know the value of the means of subsistence—food, clothing, fuel, and housing—that are required to maintain a laboring individual. In addition, however, Marx also recognized that a distinctive cultural factor influences the needs of workers:

> The number and extent of [the worker's] so-called necessary wants, as also the modes of satisfying them, are themselves the product of historical development, and depend therefore to a great extent on the degree of civilization of a country, more particularly on the conditions under which, and consequently on the habits and degree of comfort in which, the class of free laborers has been formed. In contradistinction therefore to the case of commodities, there enters into the determination of the value of labor-power a *historical and moral element* [p. 150 (emphasis added)].

Despite the difficulties of measuring the value of labor power, Marx concluded that "in a given country, at a given period, the average quantity of the means of subsistence necessary for the laborer is practically known" [p. 150]. The value of labor power is a sum of the labor of others required to keep the laborer continuously appearing in the market and the labor required to train and maintain his children, who are his future substitutes.

How much labor of others is required to reproduce the laborer from day to day? Marx speculated that it would take six hours of others' labor to do this. In monetary terms, this would come to three shillings of payment to them. This means that the wage for the work of the laborer is also three shillings, because that is the equivalent of the amount of labor that has gone into producing him. Marx treated the laborer strictly as a commodity, and the wages he receives are calculated in the same way as prices are calculated for any commodity—in terms of the labor congealed in them. The purchaser of labor power must pay three shillings, or else the labor power will deteriorate and cannot produce commodities with use values.

In this peculiar commodity of labor power Marx found the secret of capital, profits, exploitation, and class warfare.

The production of absolute surplus value. Marx first considered what he called absolute surplus value, or that type of capital that is produced *within* a given technological framework. Thus he assumed economic organization and technology to remain constant. He also made a number of other assumptions about the conditions of capitalist production and marketing. First, the worker sells his labor power, like any other commodity would be sold; the worker has no other commodity than his labor to sell; he sells it to the potential capitalist; and the product of his labors are the property of the potential capitalist.

To observe how surplus value is extracted from the worker, Marx reviewed the factors that go into the production of a given commodity, for example, cotton yarn. Pursuing a hypothetical example, he noted that the wear and tear of the spindles and other machinery, as well as the raw material that goes into the yarn, are not without value. Certain types of labor must have gone into them in order to make them useful for spinning cotton yarn. Marx calculated the value of the fixed and working capital hypothetically as two days' labor, or twelve shillings. {40} Marx was counting capital as stored-up labor, which is consumed in the process of production.

In addition to the fixed and working capital, the laborer, too, expends energy, and it is necessary to calculate how much labor has to go into him to make him reproducible for the following day. Again, Marx calculated hypothetically that six hours, or three shillings, would be required. If we add the cost of maintaining the spindles, the raw cotton, and the worker for six hours, the cotton yarn is worth fifteen shillings, and this represents the value of the labor that went into the product.

At this point the capitalist sees some possibilities. The worker requires three shillings per day to keep himself alive and reappearing in the market, and the capitalist must pay this amount. But this does not prevent the capitalist from working the laborer *more* than six hours but still paying him three shillings. The capitalist proceeds to work the worker *twelve* hours, paying him only the necessary three shillings in twelve hours. In a twelve-hour period, the capitalist pays twenty-four shillings for spindles and raw cotton, three shillings for necessary labor, but retains the three shillings that the laborer has created in use values during his excess six hours. In this way the capitalist has created three shillings for *surplus value* for himself. This is the key to production of absolute surplus value—working the worker for more hours than is necessary to keep him reappearing in the market.

To calculate the rate of surplus value, Marx made a number of formal definitions. First, he defined the spindles, machinery, building, raw cotton, as *constant capital* (*c*). It is "that part of capital which is represented by the means of production, by the raw material, auxiliary material, the instruments of labor, and does not in the process of production, undergo any quantitative alteration of value" [p. 191]. The stored-up labor in capital is transferred without modification to the final product of cotton yarn. Second, the production process also involves *variable capital (v),* which is "represented by labor power, and which does, in the process of production, undergo an alteration of value. It produces the equivalent of its own value [that necessary to keep the laborer appearing in the market] and also produces a surplus-value" [pp. 191-192]. To calculate the rate of surplus value, *c* is ignored, for it simply transfers its value to the final product. The remaining value of the final product contains a certain amount of variable capital (*v*) *and* a certain amount of surplus value (*s*). The rate of production of surplus value is the ratio of the surplus value to the variable capital:

$$\frac{s}{v}$$

In the hypothetical example above, the rate of surplus value would be arrived at by dividing three shillings (surplus value) by three shillings (variable capital); the rate of surplus value would be 1.0.[31]

On the basis of this calculation, Marx arrived at a technical definition of exploitation: "[the] rate of surplus-value is . . . an exact expression for the degree of exploitation of labor-power by capital, or of the laborer by the capitalist" [pp. 200-201]. For Marx, therefore, exploitation is not simply a general form of economic injustice. It is a technically defined process, derived from a view of the economy based on the labor theory of value. The social classes that emerge from the process of producing surplus value are also technically defined. Those classes accruing surplus value are the capitalists, or the bourgeoisie; those being exploited are the workers, or the proletarians.

Thus far, Marx's examples of surplus value have been purely hypothetical; they have been given meaning only in terms of the formal structure of his theory. How, in practice, does the capitalist acquire absolute surplus value?

Marx answered by arguing that under a given system of technology the capitalist extends the working day to extract the maximum surplus value from the worker in the minimum time. He stops short of killing the laborer by overwork, because he has an interest in seeing that the worker continues to appear in the market; but this is the only limit on the capitalist. Under the capitalist system there is an inherent tendency to extend the workday as far as possible. This tendency is to be found, moreover, wherever capitalism is found. "The production of [absolute] surplus-value . . . prove[s] to be independent of any change in the mode of production itself . . . it was not less active in the old-fashioned bakeries than in the modern cotton factories" [p. 297]. The production of absolute surplus value does not require any growth or expansion of capitalism to realize itself.

---

[31] The rate may also be stated in terms of a ratio between surplus labor and the necessary labor, or between surplus produce and necessary produce [pp. 200-213].

Counteracting the tendency of exploitation is the tendency of the laboring classes to resist the exploitation: "the laborer maintains his right as seller when he wishes to reduce the working day to one definite normal duration" [p. 218]. The history of capitalist production, then, can be read as a struggle between {41} the exploiters and the exploited. "[The] determination of what is a working day presents itself as the result of a struggle, a struggle between collective capital, i.e., the class of capitalists, and collective labor, i.e., the working class."

Having given his theory of the production of absolute value some empirical reference, Marx then turned to the facts of capitalist history and interpreted them in the light of this theory. Chapter 10 of *Capital* is devoted to an extensive documentation of the capitalists' strategies of lengthening the working day. Marx interpreted the history of labor under capitalism as a complicated interplay among three historical tendencies: (1) The tendency of capitalism "to appropriate labor during all the 24 hours of the day" [p. 241]. (2) The limitation imposed by the need to keep labor at a bare survival level in order that it continue to be available for capitalist exploitation. "[The] limiting of factory labor was dictated by the same necessity which spread guano over the English fields. The same blind eagerness for plunder that in the one case exhausted the soil, had, in the other, torn up by the roots the living force of the nation" [p. 222]. (3) The power of "the working class movement that daily grew more threatening." A major part of the history of capitalism, then, is the story of the struggle for a normal working day.

Summary and recapitulation. We have now concluded the long journey from the definition of a commodity to the explanation of some of the basic facts of capitalist production. Marx first defined the nature of a commodity in terms of value, which was found in human labor. Next, he determined the nature of capital, which is systematically extracted in the form of surplus labor from the process of circulation of commodities of labor. He then equated the rate of creation of surplus value with the rate of exploitation of workers by capitalists. Next, he identified one major form of exploitation as the extension of the working day by capitalists. He next argued, by further specification, that many critical historical events in capitalism can be interpreted as a working-out of this struggle between the exploiters and the exploited. Finally, he interpreted, at great length, events such as the imposition of night work, the relay system, and the workers' mobilization to agitate for a normal working day as the historical manifestation of this struggle.

I have not summarized Marx's theory in terms of the seven components of scientific inquiry outlined at the beginning of this essay. The exposition of that theory is complicated enough as it is, and such a summary would have encumbered the presentation. Nevertheless, it is possible to recapitulate his theory in terms of those components.

1. The basic problems that Marx faced were to identify the laws governing the production, exchange, and distribution of commodities (labor included) under the capitalist system and the relations among the various agents in this process. His range of data thus included a vast array of economic and social characteristics of the capitalist system.

2. His basic concepts were "commodity" and "labor." From these basic concepts he proceeded logically to the concepts of exchange, surplus value, exploitation, profits, and the conflict among classes.

3. Marx "operationalized" his basic concepts by a selective reading of the history of capitalism, mainly in eighteenth- and nineteenth-century Britain. The weakness of this method is found in the word "selective." By virtue of his theoretical and ideological commitments, Marx was inclined to "find" and emphasize exploitation and conflict in the complex historical literature. In my own research on the British Industrial Revolution (Smelser 1959), I read many of the same historical sources (for example the Parliamentary "blue books") as Marx, but saw in those pages many other, sometimes humanitarian patterns of capitalists' behavior that Marx passed over.

4. The structure of Marx's theory involves the logical relationship between labor, surplus value, exploitation, and the other basic concepts. Marx's theory is especially impressive in its systematic transitions from one basic concept to the next. It closely approaches derivation, because each new basic concept is defined explicitly in terms of the foregoing ones.

5. The propositions emerging from the theory are many, but the master proposition is that the capitalists, or extractors of surplus value, maximize their position by accumulating as much value (profits) as they can without actually destroying the working population. Correspondingly, the workers resist this exploitation and

demand the normal working day, which represents the true value of their labor.

6. Empirically these propositions translate into historical statements that the classes will behave as if in conflict—the capitalists to extend hours, the workers to shorten them. The result will be a series of struggles emerging from the basically antipathetic positions of the classes.

7. Marx attempted to verify these historical statements by detailed historical investigation of working conditions under the capitalist mode of production.

The production of relative surplus value. In his analysis of absolute surplus value, Marx noted that he was not considering "changes in the method of production." His analysis of the working day related only to "given conditions of production" and to "a given stage in the economical development of society" [p. 300]. After considering absolute surplus value, Marx relaxed these assumptions.

The production of *absolute* surplus value depends on establishing a ratio between surplus value and variable capital, and can be expressed in the formula s/v. Furthermore, absolute surplus value is produced by lengthening the working day and thereby making s larger.

The production of *relative* surplus value also involves {42} increasing the ratio between s and v, but it does so by making v smaller. Marx defined relative surplus value as "arising from the curtailment of the necessary labor-time, and from the corresponding alteration in the respective lengths of the two components of the working day [that is, necessary and surplus labor-time]" [p. 304].

How can necessary labor time (variable capital) be reduced? Marx found the answer in technological change, which cuts down the variable capital or necessary labor time to produce a commodity. Pursuing a hypothetical example, Marx argued that by saving labor by a mechanical invention, the capitalist lowers the cost of his commodity from one shilling to nine pence, thus giving himself three pence more surplus value than before applying the invention. Of course, the capitalist lowers his price somewhat, say to ten pence, which means that he acquires two pence less in the market for his product, but he gains a marked advantage over his competitors and still retains one pence more of surplus value than his competitors.

The production of relative surplus value means that the capitalist attains surplus value relative to other capitalists operating under less advanced technological conditions. On the basis of this reasoning, Marx concluded that "there is a motive for each individual capitalist to cheapen his commodities by increasing the productiveness of labor" [p. 307].

Of course, the innovating capitalist's advantage is likely to be temporary. As a new method of production becomes widely known, other capitalists pick it up, and the relative difference between the innovator's profits and the profits of the others begins to diminish. The capitalist system thus coerces competitors to adopt new methods and coerces prospective innovators to seek continuously for new ways to improve their relative position once again.

By improving technology and reducing the necessary part of the working day, the capitalist is simultaneously reducing the amount of labor time necessary to keep his laborers on the job. This should not suggest, however, that the capitalist actually reduces the length of the working day. In fact, Marx argued that the capitalist attempts to maximize both absolute and relative surplus value. He lengthens the working day and cuts the necessary working time at the same time. Both strategies work toward the maximization of surplus value, exploitation, and profits. The production of absolute surplus value and the production of relative surplus value are simply two different ways for the capitalist to attain his objectives.

By introducing the notion of relative surplus value, Marx made his view of the capitalist system dynamic. The capitalist innovates to gain an advantage over his competitors, because he is motivated to increase his surplus value. Furthermore, innovation is necessarily temporary, because competitors continuously copy new advances and reduce the relative advantage of the innovators. Capitalists are thus motivated to change the system of production at an increasingly furious rate. Insofar as this process of change increases the level of relative surplus value, exploitation becomes more and more severe as the capitalist system moves ahead.

What are the specific mechanisms by which the capitalist increases relative surplus value? Marx identified three such mechanisms: the introduction of cooperation among laborers; the introduction of a division of labor; and the introduction of machinery.

1. Cooperation. Marx argued that the bringing together of laborers into cooperative relationships made for a more productive enterprise (and through that an increase of relative surplus value). First, in cooperating, many workers use capital in common, and this cheapens commodities and brings about a decrease in necessary labor. It is more economical to use twenty weavers to one building than one weaver to one building. Second, working cooperatively increases the morale of each worker. Third, a pressing project (for example, the harvesting of wheat) can be completed more effectively if many cooperate. Fourth, work over an extended space can be completed more effectively through cooperation. Finally, Marx noted that increased cooperation gives rise to the possibility of an increased division of labor. Each of these effects augments relative surplus value.

As might be expected, Marx regarded cooperation as one of the manifestations of the capitalist's motive "to extract the greatest possible amount of surplus-value from the workers" [p. 321]. At the same time, he noted that cooperation and increasing productivity set the stage for a more effective resistance to this kind of exploitation on the part of the laborers.

> As the number of the cooperating laborers increases, so too does their resistance to the domination of capital, and with it, the necessity for capital to overcome this resistance by counter-pressure [discipline and control]. The control exercised by the capitalist is not only a special function, due to the nature of the social labor-process, and peculiar to that process, but it is, at the same time, a function of the exploitation of a social labor-process, and is consequently rooted in the unavoidable antagonism between the exploiter and the living and laboring raw material he exploits [p. 321].

Innovation increases exploitation, which in turn increases the antagonism of the laborers toward the {43} capitalists. This in turn increases the efforts on the part of the capitalists to overcome this antagonism.

2. Manufacturing, or the division of labor. Marx saw a similar advantage accruing to the capitalist who has workers assemble different objects into a single commodity or has them progressively modify a commodity into its final form. The economic effect of an increasing division of labor is to simplify the tasks of any one laborer, to

integrate the efforts of all, to make work more efficient, and thereby to increase the surplus value for the capitalist. Furthermore, because of the increased efficiency of labor, manufacturing imparts to the capitalist system a tendency to grow larger and larger, to expand its capital and concentrate it in fewer hands [pp. 353-354]. The social effect of the increasing division of labor is to begin the process of dividing society into two groups—a small group of intelligent persons and a large group of detailed laborers, whose relationship to the productive process becomes more and more remote. Manufacturing decomposes the handicrafts and begins to form a large army of detailed laborers. This process of destruction of skill is not completed, however, until the onset of machinery [p. 362].

3. Machinery has a much greater impact on the worker than co-operation or manufacturing, but it resembles these more modest innovations in that it is yet another way of maximizing relative surplus value for the capitalist.

For Marx, the essence of machinery consists of the substitution of natural power for human power and the application of science—as opposed to the rule of thumb—to manufacturing. The result is that manufacturing is removed from the control of the workman. Machinery enforces a pattern of cooperation on labor, but it is different from the kind that existed before machinery. "[The] co-operative character of the labor-process [under machinery] is a technical necessity, dictated by the instrument of labor itself" [p. 382].

To calculate the value of the final product under conditions of machine production, it is necessary to count the amount of labor that goes into the manufacture of the machine and compare this with the amount of current labor it saves. If the total labor entering the product is less, the capitalist has increased productivity and thereby increased his profit.

Marx specified a number of mechanisms by which machinery leads to greater exploitation, and thereby to greater antagonism among the classes. The first effect of machinery is to appropriate supplementary labor, mainly in the form of women and children, as adjuncts to the machinery. This becomes possible because of the minor cleaning, tending, and other ancillary, low-skill operations connected with the operation of machinery.

How does the employment of women and children provide the capitalist with more surplus value? It will be recalled that the labor necessary to sustain a worker in the market also includes the labor necessary to support his family so that tomorrow's labor force can be produced. In any case the capitalist has to pay the laborer sufficient wages to support his family. If the capitalist employs the worker, his wife, and his two children at the same time, he gains the work of four instead of one for the cost of supplying a family's subsistence.

The economic effect of appropriating supplementary labor is to multiply the amount of relative surplus value available to the capitalist. The social effects are equally profound. The workman becomes a slave dealer; "previously, [he] sold his own labor-power, which he disposed of nominally as a free agent. Now he sells wife and child" [p. 393]. Factory labor leads to the physical deterioration and the moral degradation of women and children. And finally, the capitalist uses women and children as a weapon in his war against male workers. "By the excessive addition of women and children to the ranks of the workers, machinery at last breaks down the resistance which the male operatives in the manufacturing period continued to oppose, the despotism of capital" [p. 400].

The second effect of machinery is to give the capitalist a new advantage in his effort to lengthen the working day. If the machine is used continuously, it can be replaced more quickly. Furthermore, most of its depreciation comes through use rather than rust and decay. In addition, the extension of the working day means more intensive use of the land, buildings, and other fixed capital. Finally, the working day can be extended, because the worker is now paced to the machine, not to his own work habits.

The further extension of the working day unfolds by two stages. First, when the entrepreneur introduces a new machine, he has a temporary monopoly, since his competitors are still producing on the old basis. During the period when profits are exceptional, the innovator attempts to build these profits as rapidly as possible, by prolonging the working day. Second, when profits begin to drop as others adopt the new technology, the capitalist lengthens the working day even more, in order to slow the decline of his profits. By such mechanisms, Marx argued, "machinery sweeps away almost every moral {44} and natural restriction on the length of the working day" [p. 406].

The third effect of machinery is to permit the capitalist to intensify labor in his factory by speeding up the machines. This strategy was adopted by capitalists, Marx argued, especially when the working class movement succeeded in reducing the absolute length of the working day in the nineteenth century.

Fourth, the introduction of machinery revolutionizes those branches that continue under old systems of production. As machinery invades capitalist production, domestic and handicraft industries either become departments of factories or are forced into increasing misery because of their inability to compete with factory-made goods. Furthermore, because of their dispersion and isolation, workers in these industries cannot resist exploitation. For these and other reasons, Marx felt that the conditions of exploitation and human degradation were at their very worst in the transitional domestic and handicraft industries [pp. 464ff.].

Finally, the introduction of machinery initiates increasingly severe crises of capitalist production. The introduction of a new method of machine production is typically followed by a brief period of extraordinarily high profits for the innovator, because of his great advantage over his competitors. As they discover his market advantage, however, they rush in great numbers to share in it. Thus capitalism grows furiously, but by bits and starts, and by recurrent crises of expansion and overproduction.

> The enormous power, inherent in the factory system, of expanding by jumps, and the dependence of that system on the markets of the world, necessarily beget feverish production, followed by overfilling of the markets, whereupon contraction of the markets brings on crippling of production. The life of modern industry becomes a series of periods of moderate activity, prosperity, overproduction, crisis and stagnation [p. 455].

The effect of these crises on the working classes is alternately to attract and to repel them from employment, generally rendering their relationship to the capitalist system more precarious. "The workpeople are . . . continuously both repelled and attracted, hustled from pillar to post . . ." [p. 456].

The capitalist, then, possesses a whole arsenal of tactics to increase exploitation—lengthening the working day, bringing workers into cooperation with one another, dividing their labor into specialized tasks, appropriating female and child labor, speeding up machinery, and the like. Moreover, the worker may be expected to resist this exploitation in whatever form he finds it. The history of class relations is therefore one of constant warfare; "[the] contest between the capitalist and the wage-laborer dates back to the very origin of capital" [p. 427]. And while Marx did not actually spell out a fixed evolution of stages of worker resistance, the development of resistance tended to parallel the development of capitalist industry.

Thus, while the class struggle "raged on throughout the whole manufacturing period" [p. 427], it took a new form with the introduction of machinery, which forcibly displaces workmen. With the introduction of machinery, the workers' attacks turned against "the instruments of labor itself," and the early history of machinery was marked by violent attacks upon new machinery [pp. 427-429].

As the excesses of exploitation by machinery multiplied in the late eighteenth century in England, and as "the workpeople learnt to distinguish between machinery and its employment by capital" [p. 429], they began to direct their attacks not so much toward the machines themselves but toward the exploitative tactics associated with them. Thus, in the early and mid-nineteenth century the workers fought to reduce the length of the working day, to reduce the labor of women and children, and to fight the tendency to speed up machinery. Marx argued that these reactions on the part of the workers were as inevitable as the introduction of machinery itself:

> Factory legislation, that first conscious and methodical reaction of society against the spontaneously developed form of the process of production is . . . just as much the necessary product of modern industry as cotton yarn, self-actors, and the electric telegraph [pp. 485- 486].

Finally, as workers develop a greater consciousness and ability to mobilize against capital, they gradually forge a revolutionary organization that is destined ultimately to overthrow the capitalist system by violence and to usher in a socialist system free from the contradictions bred by the system of capitalist production.

Some Criticisms of Marx's Theoretical Foundations of Capitalist Society

One of the remarkable features of Marx's theory, as developed in *Capital*, is its systematic series of transitions from general principles to specific historical interpretations. The first and most fundamental ingredient of his theory is the *labor theory of value*, by which he attempted to demonstrate that the value of—as well as the rates of exchange among—commodities {45} can be explained by calculating the quantity of labor that has entered into them. In accord with this general principle, Marx defined the commodity of labor and deduced that by buying and selling labor power it is possible to create *surplus value*, or the accumulation of value above and beyond that imparted to commodities. To define surplus value, moreover, is to provide the definitions of *capital, exploitation*, and *profits*, all of which are direct expressions of the process of extracting surplus value from the working population. Next, by introducing a notion of the organization of production, Marx was able to identify the *specific means* of augmenting surplus value and exploitation—means such as extending the working day, introducing machinery, recruiting women and children, and so forth. By further specification, he argued that the intensity of *class antagonism* and *class struggle* would also be a direct expression of the level of exploitation inflicted by the capitalist class, though the form of the struggle would depend on the maturity of the working-class movement as well. Having arrived at this level of specificity, Marx had produced a series of statements about how capitalists and workers would behave—the capitalists to maximize profits, surplus value, and exploitation, and the workers to resist in a variety of ways—and he could write the history of capitalism in terms of these tendencies.

We shall develop two lines of criticism of this elaborate theoretical structure. First, we shall raise a number of questions about the basic concepts Marx employed in erecting his theoretical scaffolding—concepts such as value, socially necessary labor time, simple average labor, and so on. This line of criticism will focus on the conceptual aspects of his theory. Second, we shall raise a number of critical observations concerning the power of his concepts to predict the future of capitalism and to account for the behavior of the working classes, particularly in the period of British history that commanded Marx's attention. This line of criticism will focus on some of the empirical, or historical, aspects of his theory.

The labor theory of value. Toward the end of the nineteenth century the Austrian economist Eugen von Bohm-Bawerk published a book entitled *Karl Marx and the Close of His System,* in which he raised a number of objections to Marx's logic in establishing the labor theory of value. In the first place, he questioned Marx's assumption that if commodities are to exchange they must have something in common. Bohm-Bawerk remarked that it would seem more logical to assume that some inequality between commodities would induce the exchange; "[where] equality and exact equilibrium obtain, no change is likely to disturb the balance" [1949, p. 68]. Marx himself seemed to be aware of this point, since he did qualify his concept of value by acknowledging that in order to exchange at all, commodities have to have some use value, that is, a qualitatively unique property.

According to Bohm-Bawerk, Marx erred further in moving from this questionable philosophical starting point to his search for the common factor. Marx used the argument by elimination: he excluded all "geometrical, physical, chemical, or other natural properties of the commodities" that make up their use value (even though, in the qualification just noted, these properties could not be excluded altogether). Leaving use value aside, Marx argued, "there remains in them only one other property, that of being products of labor." Bohm-Bawerk reacted sharply to this argument:

> Is it so? I ask . . . is there only one other property? Is not the property of being scarce in proportion to demand also common to all exchangeable goods? Or that they are the subjects of demand and supply? Or that they are appropriated? Or that they are natural products? . . . Or is not the property that they cause expense to their pro-ducers . . . common to exchangeable goods [1949, p. 75]?

Finally, Bohm-Bawerk criticized Marx for his discrepancy in the treatment of labor and all other commodities. Marx argued that values-in-use of all commodities are qualitatively different and cannot be compared; but with respect to labor he was prepared to separate a quantitative value-in-use (that is, the wearing down of "human brains, nerves, and muscles") from its qualitative aspect. Why could not the same distinction be made for other commodities, whose value-in-use could then be made a quantitatively comparable basis for exchange [1949, pp. 76-77]?

Bohm-Bawerk's general philosophical criticism's themselves have not gone unchallenged [Hilferding 1949], and, even if correct, do not necessarily undermine completely Marx's conclusions about the functioning of the capitalist system, which may be *empirically* valid even if not properly derived from Marx's first principles. Nevertheless, criticisms of the sort advanced by Bohm-Bawerk do raise questions about the soundness of the *logical* basis Marx advanced for accepting the fundamental premises of his theory.

Marx's equivocations on several central concepts. Equally serious—though different—logical problems arise in connection with two of Marx's attempted refinements {46} of the labor theory of value: his concept of simple average labor, and his concept of socially necessary labor time.

1. Simple average labor. Marx arrived at his notion of simple average labor by disregarding the qualitative element of labor and considering the remaining quantitative "expenditure of human brains, nerves, and muscles." The problem of diverse skills—the violinmaker and the common laborer—is handled by assuming that a reduction is made, whereby the value of the labor of the violinmaker is some multiple of that of the laborer.

How is simple average labor to be measured? By what formula should the various multiples of simple labor be calculated empirically? Marx never gave a satisfactory answer. Simple average labor cannot be calculated by observing a laborer at work and counting the absolute hours he works, because he is working with a certain level of skill and within a certain technological level. Nor can it be found in the actual level of wages paid to a laborer.[32] Simple average labor is something concealed; "[the] different proportions in which different sorts of labor are reduced to unskilled labor as their standard, are established by a social process that goes on behind the backs of the producers, and consequently, appear to be fixed by custom" [p. 12]. Nonetheless, Marx argued that experience shows that this reduction is constantly being made.

---

[32] In discussing simple average labor, Marx reminds the reader that "we are not speaking here of the wages or value that the laborer gets for a given labor-time, but of the value of the commodity in which that labor-time is materialized" [p. 12].

Given this formulation, it is difficult to know how to determine simple average labor in commodities other than by observing the ratios at which commodities actually exchange. But that exchange ratio is presumably what is to be explained by referring to the amount of labor. Marx seemed to place himself in a circle, whereby he argued that the exchange ratios are determined by the amount of simple average labor and that we know the amount of simple average labor by looking at the exchange ratios. The presumed cause is likely to be identified only by its presumed effects. Furthermore, if the amount of simple average labor cannot be identified empirically aside from exchange ratios, it tends to become simply another way of renaming whatever exchange ratios happen to exist at any given time. The concept of simple average labor, in short, is an evasive concept. Marx supplied no operations by which it might be identified empirically, and in so far as he hinted that it is to be discovered in the exchange process itself, he approached the danger of circular reasoning.

2. Socially necessary labor time. Marx qualified his concept of labor by arguing that absolute hours of labor can be considered comparable only under a given state of technology. The amount of labor time necessary to produce an article changes as technology changes. But as in the case of simple average labor, Marx provided no hints as to how the amount of socially necessary labor time could be calculated in practice. This omission is a particularly serious one, since the concept plays such a crucial role in his theory of surplus value. Surplus value, as well as exploitation, is represented as a ratio between surplus labor time divided by necessary labor time. But in his own demonstration of how surplus value is created, Marx relied not on any *empirical* measure of necessary labor time, but instead on a purely *hypothetical* representation of six hours of labor time, without defending his choice of this particular number. His entire calculation rested on this hypothetical figure; moreover, his concept of the rate of surplus value would have been drastically affected if he had chosen some number of hours—for example, twelve or thirteen—for necessary labor time, a number that could not be readily lengthened on an absolute basis. Marx did note that necessary labor includes food, fuel, housing, and other necessary wants, but that it also contains a "historical and moral element"—a complex package of inputs that appears to defy accurate measurement and calculation. In short, Marx's failure to provide empirical clues to the calculation of necessary labor time weakens his derivation of surplus value, capital, profits, and exploitation.

To summarize this line of criticism, it appears that Marx enfeebled his theory by making a number of important equivocations. First, he equivocated with respect to the principle that only labor determines exchange value by acknowledging that a minimum of use value is necessary. Second, he qualified the labor theory of value by saying that the amount of labor has to be both "simple average" and "socially necessary" in form. But in indicating how such labor might be empirically identified, he further equivocated by falling back on phrases such as "experience shows," or "it can be practically known." Such equivocations prompted E. H. Carr to venture the following harsh judgment:

> Instead of the concrete proposition that "the value of a commodity is determined by the labor-time requisite to produce it," we are now asked to believe that a certain abstract property called value, which belongs {47} to any labor-produced commodity, and which, though purporting to be its exchange-value, does not in fact coincide with its price . . . is determined by the amount embodied in the said commodity of another abstract property called "simple average labor." Stated in such terms, the labor theory of value becomes a pure abstraction. It may be believed in as a matter of faith; but it cannot be proved or disproved by logic. It may possess a moral or philosophical meaning; but whether true or false, it has ceased to have any validity in the world of economics [p. 264].

Such a judgment is overstated. It is not necessary to demand that abstract concepts correspond to reality, for concepts are meant, not simply to reflect reality, but to enhance our understanding of reality by giving us reasons to expect certain empirical outcomes under specified conditions.[33] Nevertheless, the judgment has some merit, since it indicates that Marx, by making a number of serious equivocations in defining his basic concepts, reduced his theory's ability to predict the specific values of a number of variables—such as surplus value and exploitation—that are essential to his entire theoretical structure.

---

[33] For a discussion of this function of conceptual models, see earlier "A Simple Model of Political Behavior."

Some Problems in Prediction and Historical Explanation

Predicting the future of capitalism. One strong feature of Marx's theory is that, despite the fact that it may rest on wobbly logical foundations, its conceptual ingredients are so organized that Marx was able to make definite predictions about the future of capitalism—that exploitation would intensify, that workers would be driven into increasing misery, and that they would eventually coalesce into a successful revolutionary movement. Marx's theory, then, appears to measure up well on the criterion of potential verifiability and falsifiability when compared, for example, to Parsons' theory of deviance.[34] In this section I shall review Marx's technical basis for predicting the future of capitalism, indicate a few of the ways in which his predictions proved vulnerable, and suggest a modification within Marx's theory that might improve its predictive potential.

Toward the end of the first volume of *Capital*, Marx turned to the analysis of the laws of capitalist growth and accumulation. The most important factor in this analysis is "the composition of capital and the changes it undergoes" [p. 208]. Marx defined this as the ratio between the constant capital, or the value of the means of production (c), and the variable capital, or value of labor power (v). These two concepts were employed in arriving at the original definition of surplus value.

If the composition of capital remains the same, an expansion of constant capital will automatically expand the variable capital by a fixed, corresponding amount. The impact of this type of expansion on class relations, Marx argued, is simply that "the sphere of capital's exploitation and rule merely extends with its own dimensions and the number of its subjects" [p. 631]. Under conditions of competition, however, capitalists begin to innovate and to accumulate more surplus value by reducing the amount of variable capital (v), thus increasing the composition ratio c/v. This process of "development of the productivity of social labor becomes the most powerful lever of accumulation" [p. 635]. By thus making fewer laborers produce more work, the capitalist alters the rate of relative surplus value. This leads in turn to the further concentration of capital, or the transformation of capital into fewer hands controlling more. As productivity

---

[34] For a discussion of some of the costs of incompleteness in Parsons' theory, see earlier, in the section on "Some Criticisms Regarding the Logic and Testability of Parsons' Theory."

increases, the number of laborers "falls in proportion to the mass of the means of production worked up by them" [p. 641].

Under these conditions of the changing composition of capital, an accelerating process of change is generated. Furthermore, since the variable part of capital (necessary labor) is continuously being reduced, the process begins to create a "relatively redundant population of laborers, a population of greater extent than suffices for the average needs of self-expansion of capital, and therefore a surplus-population" [pp. 643-634]. It is the essence of capitalism to form "a disposable industrial reserve army, that belongs to capital; it creates, for the changing needs of the self-expansion of capital, a mass of human material always ready for exploitation" [p. 646]. This accelerating vicious circle associated with continuing increases in productivity leads to a deterioration of the labor force and permits the continuing use of supplementary labor, replacement of skilled by unskilled workers, and so on. In the long run the contradictions bred by this law of capitalist accumulation lead to the deterioration of the entire system:

> within the capitalist system all methods for raising the social productiveness of labor are brought about at the cost of the individual laborer; all means for the development of production transform themselves into {48} means of domination over, and exploitation of, the producers; they mutilate the laborer into a fragment of a man, degrade him to the level of an appendage of a machine, destroy every remnant of charm in his work, and turn it into a hated toil; they estrange from him the intellectual potentialities of the labor-process in the same proportion as science is incorporated in it as an independent power; they distort the conditions under which he works, subject him during the labor-process to a despotism more hateful for its meanness; they transform his life-time into working-time, and drag his wife and child beneath the wheels of the juggernaut of capital. But all methods for the production of surplus-value are at the same time methods of accumulation; and every extension of accumulation becomes again a means for the development of those methods. It follows therefore that in proportion as capital accumulates, the lot of the laborer, be his payment high or low, must grow worse. The law,

finally, that always equilibrates the relative surplus-population, or industrial reserve army, to the extent and energy of accumulation, this law rivets the laborer . . . firmly to capital . . . It establishes an accumulation of misery, corresponding with accumulation of capital. Accumulation of wealth at one pole is, therefore, at the same time accumulation of misery, agony of toil, slavery, ignorance, brutality, mental degradation, at the opposite pole . . . [pp. 660-661].

Many of the criticisms of Marx in the century since *Capital* was written have taken the form that Marx was mistaken in his predictions: that capital has not centralized at the rate anticipated by Marx; that the industrial reserve army has not increased at an accelerated rate; that technology has wiped out unskilled jobs more than skilled ones; that the diversification of "proletarian" jobs has prevented the emergence of a unified working class; that gradual diminution of worker exploitation through reform instead of violent revolution has been the hallmark of the subsequent development of capitalist societies; that class conflict has been successfully institutionalized; and so on.[35]

In so far as these generalizations about the past century of the history of capitalism are accurate, they constitute important objections to Marx's theory. Instead of concluding simply that "Marx was wrong," however, or examining in detail each prediction emanating from his theory, I am going to argue that many of the valid parts of Marx's theory of capital accumulation can be accepted, despite the fact that they led to erroneous predictions. The method of making them acceptable, moreover, is to modify one critical assumption in his formulation of the law of accumulation, thereby permitting different lines of prediction to emerge from his theory.

The critical assumption has to do with a key qualification in *Capital*: that the "necessary wants" of a laborer—that is, those things that must be satisfied if a laborer is to continue to appear in the market—*are themselves subject to historical variation.* Marx explicitly acknowledged this when he said that wants "depend to a great extent on the degree of civilization of a country," and thus depend on "a

---

[35] For a development of a number of these criticisms, compare Dahrendorf 1959, ch. II.

historical and moral element" [p. 150]. Yet in his own formulation of the basic law of capital accumulation—which involves an accelerating process of reducing necessary labor time—Marx implicitly held the "necessary wants" of workers constant. In fact, however, many of the struggles of social groups in the past century have concerned the degree to which subordinated groups in Western societies "deserve" various social benefits such as education, decent housing, exposure to culture, and so on. Such struggles, which have brought about significant social changes, have concerned the cultural definitions of what is socially necessary for workers and other groups. As such, these changes have reduced the pace at which technological innovation has reduced necessary labor by changing the cultural criteria of what is necessary for labor.

If Marx had envisioned a substantial change in the cultural definition of a worker's "needs" or "wants"—that is, if he had allowed for a substantial modification in the social definition of necessary labor time—he might well have softened his predictions concerning the rate at which surplus value and profits are created, the rate at which capital is centralized, the rate at which an industrial reserve army grows, and so on. The corresponding predictions concerning the class struggle also would have been broadened to include the possibility that the bourgeoisie and the proletarians would engage in political struggles over worker's "rights"—that is, the proper social definitions of their necessary and legitimate wants and needs—as well as in life-and-death revolutionary struggles involving the fate of the whole capitalist system.

What I am suggesting is that Marx's predictions about the future of capitalism were incorrect in part because he envisioned the entire evolution of capitalism as depending only on changes in one fundamental factor: the changing composition of capital. I am suggesting further that it would be fruitful to modify this vision by permitting the possibility of variation in certain historical and moral conditions that Marx himself acknowledged as variable in principle. This theoretical modification would appear not only to make Marx's predictions more realistic {49} historically but at the same time would preserve the basically valid relations between the components of capital as analyzed by Marx.

Some problems in using "exploitation" and "class consciousness" as explanatory concepts. One of the central principles in Marx's interpretation of capitalist history is that capitalists and workers are ranged in opposition to one another and that workers will fight exploitation as they find it oppressing them.

Basing his interpretations on this principle, Marx advanced an interpretation of the behavior of the British workers in the eighteenth and nineteenth centuries in relation to the length of the working day. He described the last third of the eighteenth century as "a violent encroachment like that of an avalanche in its intensity and extent. All bounds of morals and nature, age and sex, day and night, were broken down.... Capital celebrated its orgies" [p. 264]. Exploitation was at its highest. Marx asserted further that "as soon as the working class, stunned at first by the noise and turmoil of the new system of production, recovered, in some measure, its senses, its resistance began." Exploitation was met by working-class resistance.

In my own research on the working classes during the British industrial revolution, however, a number of historical events appeared not to square with the supposed relationship between exploitation and its resistance. Working-class agitation to shorten hours and improve conditions did not appear until several decades after the bitterest exploitation of the early factory system. Furthermore, when the antagonism between capitalists and workers flared over the question of hours in the 1830's and 1840's, the conditions of exploitation—hours, wages, health, and so on—were improving. Finally, after the Factory Act of 1833 was passed, *both* workers and capitalists cooperated to evade the act, lengthen hours, overwork children, and thereby increase the level of worker exploitation. The workers' agitations throughout the 1830's display this same interest in perpetuating the system of child labor [Smelser 1959, pp. 214, 238-244].

How might Marx have accounted for these positive instances of exploitation that did not manifest themselves in worker resistance, and negative instances of diminishing workers' exploitation accompanied by opposition to the capitalists and to the government? One possibility, suggested by Marx's observation that the working class was "stunned" and required time to "recover its senses," is that for a time workers were unconscious of their position and their interests. This is a famous phenomenon of "false consciousness," or, perhaps more accurately in this case, "delayed consciousness." This kind of explanation, which takes both time and experience into account, appears to throw light on the timing of the British workers' reactions to exploitation. As general theoretical categories, however, the conceptions of "consciousness" and "false consciousness" create certain problems. Unless they are specifically related to the objective conditions of exploitation, they do not reveal precisely what kind of time lag might obtain between exploitation and resistance. These concepts themselves do not indicate why the workers waited until the 1830's to agitate, or why they did not agitate in 1800, or why they did not delay until 1850, or 1890, or even until the present. Furthermore, such categories are likely to become floating appendages to the theory of exploitation that can be used flexibly to help account *both* for occasions on which exploited workers revolt ("because they were exploited") *and* for occasions on which they do not ("because they have not become conscious of their position"). The categories of consciousness, delayed consciousness, and false consciousness, in short, may be used as elastic "residual categories" that sacrifice the explanatory power of the theory of exploitation by making it nonfalsifiable.

A second possibility, suggested by Marx's observation that workers become "slave dealers" in the labor of their wives and children under conditions of machine production, is that workers are so badly exploited that they turn to the exploitation of their dependents. Like the former, this possibility is probably documentable historically, but also like the former, it requires formal theoretical incorporation to avoid becoming a convenient explanatory "out" to be used when workers do not resist capitalist exploitation according to theoretical expectations.

In addition, the Marxian concept of exploitation itself poses certain explanatory problems. Using his own definitions of exploitative tactics, it is possible to discover clear cases of exploitation as a backdrop for British worker agitation in the 1820's and 1830's—the increase of productivity by the introduction of superior machines and the displacement of adult male laborers (the increase of relative surplus value). At the same time, however, other kinds of exploitation were apparently diminishing. The production of absolute surplus value was decreasing with the gradual diminution of hours, and real wages were rising. Which kind of exploitation do we choose to explain the agitation among the workers? And why was not the greater absolute exploitation through long hours the cause of a similar agitation earlier? Such questions arise because the Marxist conception

{50} of exploitation has many components—long hours, displacement of adult labor, overwork of females and children, and so on—the relations among which are only partially specified. It is possible to discover *some* type of exploitation at *all* times in the late eighteenth and early nineteenth centuries in Great Britain. Yet the workers engaged in class warfare only irregularly and on specific occasions. The concept of exploitation, in short, is perhaps too general and inclusive to explain the specifics of worker protests.[36]

Robert Michels' Theory of Organizational Structure

As we have just seen, one of Marx's most conspicuous characteristics was his profound antagonism toward industrial capitalism. He regarded it as an economic system that set classes of men in conflict with one another and generated the conditions for its own downfall by means of revolutionary overthrow. Marx's sympathies, moreover, lay with the proletarian class, which would mobilize and overturn the political and economic structure of capitalist society and build the foundations for the communism of the future.

Robert Michels, born in 1876—shortly after the publication of *Das Kapital*—was thoroughly exposed to Marxism and he shared many of the revolutionary ideals of Marxist socialism. His great contribution to sociology, *Political Parties,* clearly shows the influence of Marx. Michels was preoccupied with the class struggle and with the kinds of organizations—trade unions, socialist political parties, cooperative societies—that represent the efforts of the workers to protest against the oppressive system of industrial capitalism.

Michels shared another characteristic with Marx. Both men tended to minimize the importance of ideas as moving forces in history. For Marx, human consciousness reflects more fundamental economic forces in society and men's ideas are determined in large part by their position in the economic system. Michels, too, regarded ideas and ideologies as rationalizations, or efforts to preserve a position of power in a social organization. The real basis for action, according to Michels, lies in the political relations among persons.

---

[36] For an elaboration of this and other criticisms of various explanations of British working-class history, see Smelser 1959, ch. XIV.

Even though Michels took up many aspects of Marxian thought, there are a number of important differences between the two men. First, Michels never intended to develop a grand, deductive theory with a full exposition of its philosophical foundations. In fact, he explicitly disavowed an interest in such theories. In the preface to *Political Parties*, he stated:

> The present study makes no attempt to offer a "new system." It is not the principal aim of science to create systems, but rather to promote understanding. It is not the purpose of sociological science to discover, or re-discover solutions, since numerous problems of the individual life and the life of social groups are not capable of "solution" at all, but must ever remain "open." The sociologist should aim rather at the dispassionate exposition of tendencies and counter-operating forces, of reasons and opposing reasons, at the display, in a word, of the warp and the woof of social life. Precise diagnosis is the logical and indispensible preliminary to any possible prognosis [p. viii].[37]

By adopting this position Michels clearly eschewed the creation of a grand theoretical and ethical system, to which Marx devoted so much of his energy. Nevertheless, as we shall see, most of the components of a theory are to be found in Michels' work; and in fact he did generate a highly organized explanation of the origins of oligarchy in social life. Second, Michels' focus was narrower than that of Marx. In particular, he was concerned with the political aspects of Marxian theory—especially class conflict between the bourgeoisie and proletariat. Michels, however, took class conflict as his starting point, whereas Marx analyzed the economic relations that give rise to class conflict. Michels concentrated on the political fate of revolutionary movements and organizations, whereas Marx built a theory that would encompass all of social life. Third, while Marx felt that in-dustrial capitalism—as well as all preceding economic systems—rendered social democracy impossible, he did predict that when the economic conditions of capitalism were destroyed and socialist so-ciety created, genuine social democracy would exist. Michels was more pessimistic. He felt that certain fundamental sociological laws

---

[37] Unless otherwise indicated, page references in brackets in this section are to Michels' *Political Parties*.

prohibited the attainment of social equality, no matter what the economic or political system. In sharp opposition to Marx, Michels argued that a socialist revolution could not substantially modify the conditions of social inequality. "The socialists might conquer, but not socialism, which would perish in the moment of its adherents' triumph. We are tempted to speak of this process as a tragicomedy in which the masses {51} are content to devote all their energies to affecting a change of masters" [p. 391].

Why did Michels lack faith in the ability of a revolutionary movement to establish a society based on social equality? To ask this question is to go to the heart of Michels' theory. Let us now recapitulate his main arguments.

A Selective Summary of Michels' Theory

The range of data and the problem. Michels' fundamental range of data can be identified empirically with two branches of the working-class movement in Europe in the late nineteenth and early twentieth centuries—socialist political parties and left-wing labor unions. He posed two sorts of questions about these organizations: (1) Why were these working class organizations ineffective in class warfare? Why had they lost their militancy? (2) Why had these organizations become less democratic? Why had leaders consolidated their positions of power? These two sets of questions were intimately connected, for in answering them Michels felt that the disappearance of democracy was one of the main factors in making such groups less militant and therefore less effective in fighting the class war.

Why did Michels choose revolutionary groups as his main object of analysis? He felt it would be too easy to choose organizations committed to oligarchic ideologies to demonstrate the universality of his new law that oligarchy arises in all organizations. He felt that revolutionary parties, committed to an ideal of egalitarianism, would be the best setting for demonstrating his law, because in such organizations it would hold *in spite of* their ideologies. "The appearance of oligarchical phenomena in the very bosom of the revolutionary parties is a conclusive proof of the existence of immanent oligarchial tendencies in every kind of human organization which strives for the attainment of definite ends" [p. 11]. Just as Durkheim chose what might appear to common sense to be the *least* social of all activities—

110

suicide—to prove the importance of the social factor, so Michels chose the type of organization apparently *least* committed to an oligarchic ideology to demonstrate the tendency for oligarchy to develop in organizations.

Central concepts. Michels' central interest is in the paired opposite concepts of oligarchy and democracy. In the history of political thought a great many meanings have been assigned to these terms, but Michels did not clearly indicate which meanings he intended to stress. Oligarchy, for example, can refer to differential participation in decision making; differential placement in power positions; differential consolidation of power over long periods of time; or exploitation of a group that does not hold power by a group that does. Michels referred to all of these meanings, and possibly more, as he developed his argument. As we shall see, a number of criticisms arise from ambiguities in his conceptualization of oligarchy and its opposite, democracy.

Michels set for himself the task of analyzing the antidemocratic tendencies in social life. Among these tendencies he singled out for special attention what he called "the nature of organization" and "the nature of the human individual" [p. viii].

Michels was also vague about the exact meaning of "organization." The term was never formally defined, and in fact Michels did not go beyond identifying certain empirical characteristics of the organization of those groups he was studying. Several salient characteristics of organization occupied his attention. The first is size. On the whole, Michels was interested in analyzing the structure of large groups, numbering perhaps from 1,000 to 10,000 members. The second is the complexity of organization—the number of functions, or degree of specialization. Third, Michels considered the coordination of group activities an important feature of organization. In these three characteristics of organization lie those tendencies that Michels believed to operate against democracy.

Michels also felt that certain psychological tendencies on the part of leaders and followers are important in the creation of oligarchic structures. He referred to age, experience, and training as important factors in leadership, and he also employed certain psychological generalizations relating to the susceptibility of the masses to persuasion and manipulation.

Operationalization. At present we shall say only a word about how Michels identified his basic concepts empirically. Like Parsons and Marx, he referred in a somewhat unsystematic way to available historical and institutional data. Michels assembled as much material as was available to him on the political parties and trade unions of his day and interpreted this information as evidence for his basic propositions. As we have seen from previous critiques, however, selective illustration is a method that may have severe limitations. We shall take up some special problems in Michels later.

Logical structure. In identifying the main tendencies that bear on democracy and oligarchy, we have already indicated a certain causal priority in {52} Michels' concepts. To formalize this priority, it is helpful to employ the language of dependent and independent variables.

The basic dependent variable in Michels' system is the degree of democracy or its opposite, oligarchy, that exists in an organization. In particular, Michels was interested in analyzing why organizations with a fighting spirit and a democratic structure gradually develop oligarchical structures over time.

All the other variables in Michels' theory can be considered as independent; and all work toward the same result. The most important independent variables are to be found in the phenomenon of organization itself. Michels referred to the "mechanical and technical impossibility of direct government by the masses" in the kinds of organizations he was analyzing [p. 226]. Several features of large organizations prevent such democratic participation. For example, large numbers of persons cannot deliberate and arrive at any sort of resolution or direct action. In addition, the masses cannot possibly participate equally in day-to-day activities of large organizations. The difficulties of maintaining adequate communication and coordination prevent the involvement of all members equally. As a result of this necessarily differential level of participation, Michels concluded that "the technical specialization that inevitably results from all extensive organization renders necessary what is called expert leadership" [p. 31]. Such are the origins of centralized power and oligarchy.

Furthermore, when a revolutionary organization begins to engage in a struggle, a hierarchical chain of command is required to mobilize the participants for action. If leaders had to consult with the rank and file on every question of action, "an enormous loss of time" would be involved, "and the opinion thus obtained would, moreover, be summary and vague" [p. 42]. Democracy is a luxury a fighting organization cannot afford.

> The problems of the hour need a speedy decision, and this is why democracy can no longer function in its primitive and genuine form, unless the policy pursued is to be temporizing, involving a loss of the most favorable opportunities for action. Under such guidance, the party becomes incapable of acting in alliance with others and loses its political elasticity. A fighting party needs a hierarchical structure [p. 42].

The very act of entering into a struggle, then, sets tendencies into play that undermine democracy in a fighting group.

Michels also considered that the psychological characteristics of the masses contribute to oligarchy. He spoke of "the need for leadership felt by the masses" [p. 49], of the "gratitude felt by the crowd for those who speak and write on their behalf" [p. 60], and of the "childish character of proletarian psychology" [p. 67]. The masses are hypnotized by a speaker's power and momentarily see in him a magnified image of their own egos. They want to have a leader they can admire and worship. "Though it grumbles occasionally, the majority is really delighted to find persons who will take the trouble to look after its affairs. In the mass, and even in the organized mass of labor parties, there is an immense need for direction and guidance" [p. 53].

Michels identified two additional peculiarities of the masses that contribute to their passivity. First, most trade union members appeared to be between the ages of 25 and 39 years [p. 78]. Michels concluded from these data that the very young men, who would supply passion to the movement, are slow to join, and men over 40 often become "weary and disillusioned" and resign their membership. "Consequently, there is lacking in the organization the force of control of ardent and irreverent youth and also that of experienced maturity." Second, the rank and file in trade unions has a more fluctuating membership than leaders, and consequently, leaders "constitute a more stable, and more constant element of the organized membership" [p. 79].

The third set of factors contributing to the development and consolidation of oligarchy comprises the qualities of individuals who become leaders. In the early stages of organization, oratorical skill is especially important; the masses are hypnotized by it. Other qualities that facilitate leaders are:

> force of will which reduces to obedience less powerful wills . . . a wider extent of knowledge which impresses the members of the leaders' environment; a catonian strength of conviction of force of ideas often verging on its very intensity; self-sufficiency, even if it is accompanied by an arrogant pride, so long as the leader knows how to make the crowd share his own pride in himself; in exceptional cases, finally, goodness of heart and disinterestedness, qualities which recall in the minds of the crowd the figure of Christ, and reawaken religious sentiments which are decayed but not extinct . . . and the prestige of celebrity [p. 72].

All three sets of independent variables work in one direction: to establish an oligarchical structure. Oligarchy, once established, moreover, has similar consequences. In particular, Michels pointed out the tendency for leaders to become superior in education, wealth, and cultural skills, once they had attained the advantages of office. In addition, leaders come to think of themselves as indispensable and {53} regard their right to office as necessary and sacred. These byproducts of oligarchical leadership feed back and further consolidate the original tendencies for power to become centralized.

The system of variables summarized in figure 13 shows how oligarchy is "overdetermined" in Michels' analysis. Everything operates in the same direction. There are no other possible outcomes; there are no important countertendencies. Given large organizations, the inevitable result is oligarchy.

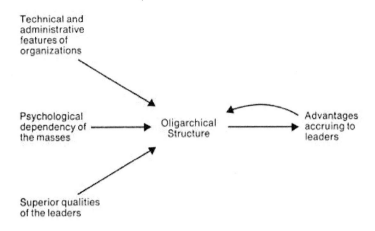

Figure 13. Causal relations among Michels' major variables.

Concluding his analysis, Michels simplified his explanation even more. In reflecting on the various forces working toward oligarchy, he observed, "now, if we leave out of consideration the tendency of the leaders, and the general immobility and passivity of the masses, we are led to conclude that the principal cause of oligarchy in the democratic parties is to be found in the technical indispensability of leadership" [p. 400]. In other words, Michels' opinion was that even if we ignore the psychological characteristics of the leaders and the led, the technical and practical features of organization are still sufficient to produce oligarchy.

Generation of hypotheses. Michels' central proposition—the iron law of oligarchy—emerges from his analysis almost as an anticlimax. Given the overdetermined explanatory scheme, there can be no other result than oligarchy. It is not surprising he called it an iron law. As Michels stated the law, "it is organization which gives birth to the dominion of the elected over the electors, of the mandataries over the mandators, of the delegates over the delegators. Who says organization, says oligarchy" [p. 401]. Michels also concluded that this law is devastating in its consequences for revolutionary movements. Only in the beginning stages can protest movements be truly fighting, democratic units. In time, however, power is consolidated, oligarchy emerges, the "embourgeoisement" of the leaders occurs, and the movements become conservative.

Empirical aspects of the study. Most of Michels' book is an effort to document his iron law by referring to the history of left-wing parties and trade unions in Europe. Basically, his method is that of selective historical comparison, not unlike that employed by Marx. In addition, Michels devoted much attention to certain facts that might have appeared to be exceptions or contradictions to his iron law. For example, he noted that proletarian leaders are sometimes substituted for bourgeois leaders in the working-class movement. But he discarded this phenomenon as offering "no guarantee, either in theory or practice, against the political or moral infidelity of the leaders" [p. 307].

In a similar spirit, Michels also developed a brief analysis of the referendum. On first glance, the referendum would appear to be a means by which the masses exercise some control over the legislation of their leaders. Yet Michels stressed the futility of the referendum and the impotence of those who try to utilize it as a political weapon. In fact, he concluded that "the history of the referendum as a democratic expedient utilized by the social parties may be summed up by saying that its application has been rare, and that its results have been unfortunate" [p. 335].

Again, on the face of it, the phenomenon of the resignation of leaders in times of crisis would seem to present evidence that the leader's power can be diminished. Michels disagreed. He argued that we should not take seriously the reasons given by leaders who resign. Rather, he interpreted the threat to resign as the leader's attempt to consolidate his own power; it is an invitation for a new mandate. The leader emphasizes his indispensability by resigning or threatening to do so, and his followers reinstate him in recognition of his indispensability. Resignation, then, is an instrument for bullying the masses and reconsolidating power.

Finally, Michels continually reiterated his position that ideology has no effect on the iron law of oligarchy. Those espousing radical syndicalist ideologies, for example, are not "immunized against the action of sociological laws of universal validity" [p. 347]. Anarchism, too, "succumbs . . . to the law of authoritarianism as soon as it abandons the region of pure thought and as soon as its adherents unite to form associations aiming at any sort of political activity" [p. 360]. {54}

In these efforts to discount possibly contrary evidence or arguments, Michels was employing a strategy that is by now familiar to us:

argument by elimination. His particular method of pressing this strategy was to acknowledge the existence of apparently contrary facts, but to deny their significance by endowing them with a meaning different from their apparent one. Michels went behind the scenes in an attempt to discover other, more fundamental mechanisms that render the superficially democratic features of organized life unimportant.

Concluding note. At the end of his analysis, Michels found himself facing a troublesome dilemma. He was a man committed to the ideals of socialist democracy, yet his discoveries seemed to have led him to the conclusion that socialist democracy is impossible. Even the class struggle would "invariably culminate in the creation of new oligarchies which undergo fusion with the old" [p. 390]. Such a discovery was no doubt extremely disquieting.

At the very end of the book Michels made an effort to restore some of his old faith. He reminded the reader that he did not wish to deny that "every revolutionary working class movement, and every movement sincerely inspired by the democratic spirit, may have a certain value as contributing to the enfeeblement of oligarchic tendencies" [p. 405]. He then related a fable: "A peasant when on his death bed tells his sons that a treasure is buried in the field. After his death they dig everywhere looking for the treasure. They do not succeed in finding it, but their indefatigable labor so improves the soil that it secures for them a comparative well-being." Michels continued: "The treasure in the fable may well symbolize democracy. Democracy is a treasure which no one will ever discover by deliberate search, but in continuing the search, in laboring indefatigably to discover the in discoverable, we shall perform a work which will have fertile results in the democratic sense" [p. 405]. Such an ending strikes a note of pathos; it seems neither realistic nor satisfactory. It is difficult to imagine a socialist party with the motto "We shall prevail, indirectly." Yet the fable and the moral that Michels drew from it perhaps constitute his own effort to reconcile his discovery of the iron law with his commitment to socialist ideals.

Some Unresolved Problems in Michels' Analysis

The conception of democracy. The model of democracy Michels adopted is an extreme one: the model of equal participation by all individuals in the decisions and binding actions of the group. Let us, however, consider another notion of democracy, one that does involve the influence of the rank and file on decision making but that does not necessarily imply equal participation by all individuals in all decisions. This alternative conception of democracy involves a plurality of organized groups, each possessing something like an oligarchical structure itself, to be sure, but each capable of exerting some power on the political center, thus representing the several groups of constituents in decision making. There is not equal participation by all, but democracy exists in the sense that the desires, grievances, and influence of the masses are taken into account when decisions are made. I am suggesting that because Michels began with an extremely individualistic notion of democracy he made his task of demonstrating that democracy could not exist in large organizations very easy; if he had considered the group-influence conception of democracy, his task would have been more complicated.

Michels also relied on the assumption that the only effective *group* for achieving democratic results is the fighting revolutionary group. When it becomes bureaucratized and conservatized, however, it loses its fighting qualities and can no longer contribute to the struggle for democracy. This assumption is contained in the following statement:

> [When a party begins to compromise with other elements in society], not merely does the party sacrifice its political virginity, by entering into promiscuous relationships with the most heterogeneous political elements, relationships which in many cases have disastrous and enduring consequences, but it exposes itself in addition to the risk of losing its essential character as a party. The term "party" presupposes that among the individual components of the party there should exist a harmonious direction of wills toward identical objectives and practical aims. Where this is lacking, the party becomes a mere "organization" [p. 376].

Linking these two key assumptions, Michels believed that democracy is impossible in large organizations, and as large organizations become undemocratic, they cannot contribute to democracy in the larger society.

I should like to raise the question of whether these two assumptions should be linked in the way that Michels linked them. I shall do so by considering an illustrative example: the history of protest movements among American farmers. In the last three decades of the nineteenth century, American farmers, suffering under great economic hardship, organized themselves into a number of "fighting" organizations, such {55} as the Grange, the Farmer's Alliance, and the Populist movement (though these organizations were not revolutionary in the same sense as European socialist groups). In this early phase of farmer protest, these groups were burdened with difficulties of recruitment, commitment, and coordination and were notoriously ineffective politically. It was only after the American farmer became involved, not in parties, but in organizations—that is, when he sacrificed his political virginity and began dealing in the world of compromise and pressure politics—that he and his organizations really began to influence governmental policy. If democracy is measured by the flow of influence from bottom to top, the mobilization of American farmers into organizations rather than parties clearly increased their democratic effectiveness. The same sort of argument might be made for the history of American labor unions. What I am suggesting by such illustrations is that in many cases Michels' iron law of oligarchy might hold *within* organizations, but the very development of this kind of leadership might equip those organizations to represent the desires and wishes of their constituents more effectively in the larger society, thus contributing to democracy at another level.

This line of reasoning suggests that in conceptualizing democracy, Michels perhaps considered too few of its aspects. At other times, however, one gains the impression that he fused too many aspects of a phenomenon into a single category. Consider the numerous connotations of the concept of oligarchy, for example. It may suggest a minority giving orders to a majority, with the majority submitting. It may connote that the minority of leaders are the sole source of any significant political action. It may mean that the minority of leaders are free from control by others who hold subsidiary positions in the organization. It may suggest that people in positions of authority pursue their own interests and exploit the others in the organization.

Or, finally, it may refer to the tendency for leaders to consolidate their positions of power over long periods of time [Cassenelli 1953].

As Michels developed his argument, he tended to slip back and forth among these several connotations. But surely the causes of the consolidation of an elite over long periods are different from the causes of temporary domination or exploitation. By not discriminating among these different aspects of oligarchy, Michels fell into the difficulty of trying to account for more facets of oligarchy than he could legitimately hope to within his relatively simple analytic framework. If the several aspects of oligarchy were sorted out from one another analytically, Michels would have been in a better position to account for each aspect by using different combinations of causes.

The uncertain status of psychological categories, especially "ideas." As indicated, Michels' work falls clearly into that tradition of thought that emphasizes "real factors"—especially economic and political—as the determinants of behavior and minimizes the influence of ideas as determining factors. Michels' repeated assertion that socialist, syndicalist, and anarchist ideologies have no significant deterrent influence on the development of oligarchic tendencies within organizations is consistent with this perspective. Also, in summing up his ideas on the origins of oligarchy, Michels concluded that the technical features of organization are a sufficient cause of oligarchic leadership and that the psychological characteristics of the masses and the leaders are only accessory and contributing factors. In all these arguments, psychological variables such as ideas and sentiments are dominated by "objective conditions."

From time to time, however, Michels appeared not quite certain how far he wished to downgrade ideas and sentiments. He entitled an early chapter "The Ethical Embellishment of Social Struggles," which suggests that the moral aspects of conflict are in the nature of unnecessary adornments. Yet in discussing the ethical side of political life, Michels spoke of the need of all political movements to develop an ideology of democracy as "a *necessary* fiction" [p. 15, emphasis added]. "Political parties, however much they may be founded upon narrow class interest and however evidently they may work against the interests of the majority, love to identify themselves with the universe, or at least present themselves as cooperating with all the citizens of the state, and to proclaim that they are fighting in the name of all and for the good of all" [p. 16]. Struggles within parties also involve appeals to ideas. "In the struggle among leaders," Michels noted, "an appeal is often made to loftier motives. When the members of the executive claim the right to intervene in the democratic functions of the individual sections of the organization, they base this claim upon their more comprehensive grasp of all the circumstances of the case, their profounder insight, their superior socialist culture, and their keener socialist sentiment" [p. 172].

In connection with these observations, we might raise a question: why should the struggle for power—which in the last analysis depends on real factors—have to be legitimized by reference to the values or beliefs of the group itself? If the struggle is essentially {56} based on power, why should not the contestants in this struggle feel free to ignore ideological questions? While Michels explicitly minimized ideological factors, his observations indicate that he believed the appeal to ideology to be an important weapon in securing the support of the masses in the drive for power. In short, Michels was ambivalent about the importance of ideas, sometimes treating them as sham and rationalization, at other times recognizing them as important and probably necessary ingredients in the struggle among groups.

A final ambiguity in Michels' discussion of human psychology lies in his treatment of certain psychological forces as both causes and effects. In discussing the "accessory qualities" of leaders, which contribute to their rise to leadership, Michels mentioned the leaders' wider extent of knowledge, their strength of conviction, the force of their ideas, their pride, and their dedication. But elsewhere in his analysis, these same qualities turn out to be the consequences of leadership as well; for example, the longer a leader remains in power, the stronger is his conviction of his own moral correctness, the greater is his self-adulation, the greater is his sense of indispensability.

Certainly it is plausible to organize one's variables into a kind of model whereby a single type of variable becomes first a cause, then an effect generated by the very set of conditions it contributed to causing in the first place. Such a model is often referred to as a "positive feedback" model. Michels made use of such a model—though it is only implicit—in his characterization of the causes of oligarchy. Yet in his own examination of the historical material, he was able to point only to the empirical correlation between the leader's position in an organization and his psychological characteristics. There is no way in which Michels could demonstrate the ways in which these psychological characteristics are simultaneously both causes and effects, given the historical data available to him.

The use of cultural differences as a residual category. Most of Michels' energies were devoted to eliciting examples of situations that confirm his iron law of oligarchy. In chapters 5-8 of Part One of *Political Parties*, for example, he selected telling examples of the psychological submission of the masses to authorities. Often, however, he noted an apparent exception to the iron law, which he tended to attribute to a specifically national or cultural factor.

For example, in discussing the stability of leadership, Michels ventured the following observation about England:

> In international European politics, England has always been regarded as an untrustworthy ally, for her history shows that no other country has ever been able to confide in agreements concluded with England. The reason is to be found in this, that the foreign policy of the United Kingdom is largely dependent upon the party in power, and party changes occur with considerable rapidity. Similarly, the party that changes its leaders too often runs the risk of finding itself unable to contract useful alliances at an opportune moment. The two gravest defects of genuine democracy, its lack of stability . . . and its difficulty of mobilization, are dependent on the recognized right of the sovereign masses to take part in the management of their own affairs [p. 103].

Thus democracy in England appeared to interfere with the conduct of foreign affairs. But England, like all advanced industrial societies, presumably had its share of large organizations, which should have been governed by the iron law of oligarchy as much as other advanced states. If the law were as universal as Michels maintained, the English exception should be an embarrassing instance for his theory. But he merely noted it as a national exception.

Discussing the tendency of leadership to consolidate, Michels made the expected assertion that "with the institution of leadership there simultaneously begins, owing to the long tenure of office, the transformation of the leaders into a closed caste" [p. 156]. Yet in the next paragraph he qualified the assertion: "Unless, as in France, extreme individualism and fanatical political dogmatism stand in the way, the old leaders present themselves to the masses as a compact phalanx—at any rate whenever the masses are so much aroused as to endanger the position of leaders." Here he was identifying something characteristically "French" that made for an exception to the iron law. In another place, he noted the presence of an abundance of Jews among the leaders of the socialist and revolutionary parties and added that "specific racial qualities make the Jew a born leader of the masses, a born organizer and propagandist" [p. 258]. Then he proceeded to detail these specifically Jewish qualities. From Michels' statements it would appear that something distinctively cultural—something associated with Jewishness—would have to do with consolidation of power above and beyond the tendencies inherent in organization itself. Yet Michels tended to leave unanalyzed both these exceptions and the implicit cultural variables that would explain them. These variables surround his theory as convenient categories that are used to add to, or to account for, apparent exceptions to the iron law. This method of proceeding gives his theory an appearance of simplicity and neatness, whereas in {57} reality he was relying on many more variables than were incorporated into his original formulation of the empirical universal.

A critical but unexamined residual category: conflict among leaders. Let us return for a moment to figure 13, in which the system of technical requisites, psychological factors, accessory qualities, and positive feedback guarantee that oligarchy is the universal consequence of organization. One implication of this explanatory scheme is that if leaders and masses come into conflict with one another, the leaders will win every time, because they command more power; there is nothing in Michels' theory to suggest otherwise. In fact, Michels is explicit: "When there is a struggle between the leaders and the masses, the former are always victorious" [p. 157].

Immediately after this statement, however, Michels added the qualifying phrase "if only they [the leaders] remain united." This suggests the possibility of victory on the part of the masses if their struggle with the leaders coincides with a struggle among the leaders themselves. His qualification further suggests two questions: (1) Why should conflict between leaders occur at all? (2) Does not a victory of the masses in periods of conflict among leaders actually constitute the exercise of democracy? Even more, if conflict among leaders is institutionalized politically, does this not make for a periodic voice of the masses and hence a periodic exercise of democracy, which would thereby qualify, if not contradict, the iron law of oligarchy?

Given the accumulation of independent variables and secondary consequences in Michels' theory, there seems to be no reason why leaders in an organization would ever come into conflict with one another. After all, as leaders they are securely placed, psychologically gratified, possessed of information, cultural accessories, and wealth, and fortified with beliefs in their indispensability. Why endanger these positions by struggling with one another? The only conflicts in Michels' theory would seem to be between those aspiring to power and those holding it, and the cards are so stacked against the former that they would always lose.

Actually, Michels presented a number of reasons why conflicts among leaders arise in organizations. He spoke of "rivalry between established leaders and great outsiders who have established reputations in other fields and then offer their services to socialist parties"; of conflict between age and youth; of conflict between leaders of bourgeois origin and leaders of proletarian origin; of struggles between subdivisions of the organization, for example, executive versus administrative, local versus national, and so forth; of struggles based on racial (i.e., ethnic) differences, for example, the contests between French and German socialists during the Franco-Prussian War of 1870; and finally, he spoke of struggles based on "objective differences and differences of principle in general philosophical views" [p. 167].

Empirically, these bases for contests among leaders make sense, and it is possible to find illustrations of each from our own knowledge of political conflict. But from a theoretical point of view, *these contests are not a consequence of the major variables in Michels' original theory.* He made no formal use of age, locality, race, ideology, and so on, except occasionally to declare one or another of them irrelevant to the iron law of oligarchy. Thus it appears that in this case, as in others, Michels introduced a number of categories that do not find a place in his original theory, but which he used to develop his argument.

Nevertheless, given *some* basis for conflict among leaders, what are the implications of this kind of conflict for the workings of democracy? Michels did give a certain power to the mass to influence factional struggles. He observed, for example, that "the path of the new aspirants to power is always beset with difficulties, bestrewn with obstacles of all kinds, *which can be overcome only by the favor of the masses*" [p. 177, emphasis added]. Apparently, then, mass support is needed for an emerging leader to overthrow an established one. Having acknowledged this, however, Michels later minimized the importance of this phenomenon by noting that:

> only in exceptional instances do [overthrows of leaders] signify that the masses have been stronger than the leaders. As a rule, they mean merely that a new leader has entered into conflict with the old, and thanks to the support of the mass, has prevailed in the struggle, and has been able to dispossess and replace the old leader. The profit for democracy of such a substitution is practically nil [pp. 182-183].

Once again, Michels' argument appears to rest on a limited view of democracy. He regarded the *fact* of leadership and followership as antipathetic to democracy. But it is also plausible to regard the overthrow of leaders—which is dependent upon mass support—as evidence of a periodic upward flow of influence. The masses will obviously support the aspiring leader who best represents what they desire. And if he ceases to take into consideration their feelings, they will be inclined to throw their support behind another contending leader.

Furthermore, if conflict among leaders is institutionalized—as in the constitutional provision for free {58} elections involving two or more parties and associated civil liberties and rights—the political system has regularized the struggle among leaders and increased the ability of the masses to express their preferences. This is not to say that the leaders will not consolidate their positions repeatedly, as Michels' analysis suggests they will do. But it is also possible to institutionalize tendencies that operate to diminish the workings of the iron law of oligarchy. The institutionalization of conflict among political leaders would seem to require a formulation of the law of oligarchy somewhat less rigid than Michels' version.

Summary and Conclusions

The Character of Theoretical Criticism in Sociology

Academic disciplines may be compared with one another according to their degree of conceptual unification. At the one extreme a discipline may possess a more or less unified paradigm, or set of organizing assumptions, on which there is broad consensus, and within which specific theoretical and empirical problems are selected for analysis. Classical physics and much of contemporary economics are illustrations of this extreme. At the other extreme a discipline may possess a number of partially developed paradigms and perspectives that are related to one another only loosely and unsystematically. The study of history is an illustration.

Sociology falls at some middle point between these extremes. On the one hand, there is fairly widespread consensus on the central concepts of the discipline- concepts such as social interaction, role, group, norm, institution, culture, and social structure—and on the canons by which theoretical and empirical knowledge is to be judged. On the other hand, the discipline is also characterized by many debates concerning its fundamental objectives, the most appropriate perspectives around which to organize sociological knowledge, and the nature of sociological knowledge itself. Sociologists debate, for example, whether their field should aim to become an objective science with little regard for practical applications or whether it should be devoted primarily to meeting social crises and promoting social change. They debate the merits of the integrationist perspective, the conflict perspective, the symbolic interactionist perspective, and others, as the most fruitful organizing paradigms for the field. And they debate the merits of different methods of arriving at sociological truths—by experimentation, by sample survey, by participant observation and empathic understanding, and so on.

Given this circumstance, it comes as no surprise that theoretical discourse takes a variety of forms in sociology. Sometimes it takes the form of advocating a particular moral, political, or epistemological perspective in favor of alternative perspectives. Durkheim's polemic in favor of positivism as a method of inquiry and in favor of "the social" as an indispensable analytic level are examples of this kind of theoretical statement. Another example is Karl Marx's advocacy of scientific socialism as a superior intellectual position to Utopian and other versions of socialist thought [1848]. Still another example is the contemporary controversy in which some sociologists argue that the field should be made "relevant" to the eradication of social and political evils facing society, some argue for a neutral, scientific posture, while others combine these arguments.

A second form of theoretical discourse involves the analysis of the history of ideas. It places the contributions of a given theorist or school of thought in relation to the dominant intellectual and cultural traditions of the time. The historian of ideas seeks out the dominant positive and negative influences on a theorist; he asks whose ideas were adopted and refashioned and whose ideas were polemically rejected by a theorist. He may also trace the impact of a given theorist or school of thought on subsequent intellectual and social developments.

A third form of theoretical discourse—the one stressed in this essay—involves the critical application of the canons of scientific adequacy to a theory. Using this approach, the theoretical critic asks what problem a given theorist has set for himself, how he organizes concepts to generate explanations relating to this problem, and how he attempts to demonstrate the validity of these explanations. This approach is clearly a normative one, because it asks how well a given theory measures up to the norms of logico-empirical inquiry as these have developed in the social sciences.

Each of these forms of theoretical discourse has a legitimate place in sociology. It is advisable, moreover, to permit each form of discourse to stand or fall on its own merits, not to let one form serve for all. For example, it is illegitimate to conclude from the observation that a theorist has a "Marxist" or a "conservative" perspective that his work is somehow unacceptable scientifically. The scientific adequacy of a work should be established by examining the logical and empirical procedures employed, not by merely identifying a perspective or "bias." Likewise, it is illegitimate to conclude that scientific criticism disposes of all aspects of a theory and that, once its {59} scientific adequacy or inadequacy has been established, no further explorations of the moral, political, or epistemological implications of the theory need be made. These two practices—the first might be called "bias-hunting," the second "scientism"—resemble one another in that each combines several independent types of criticism into a single line of criticism, thereby overextending and overworking it.

Furthermore, any given theory may be "important" or "influential" or "good" for a variety of different reasons, of which its scientific adequacy is only one. The theories we have considered, for example, have attained historical importance because each was a novel, creative, or forceful formulation of the relationships among basic sociological variables, and also because each, in a different way, addressed an especially critical set of social and political issues facing human society—issues such as social integration, social control, conflict, social domination, and so on. To undertake the logico-empirical criticism of a theory, then, is not to assess its entire value, but only selected aspects of its value.

Finally, the scientific form of theoretical criticism emphasizes the form of a theory more than its content. It focuses on a theorist's procedures rather than on the substantive implications of his conclusions. Nevertheless, it is possible, even in authors so diverse as the ones we have considered, to note the emergence of common substantive themes. Each, for example, recognized the social importance of committed, organized groups of people pursuing a cause, though each emphasized different aspects of such groups. Durkheim saw them as providing cohesive bonds that counteracted individual tendencies to self-destruction; Parsons regarded them as a setting in which both sides of the ambivalence involved in deviance can be gratified; Marx treated them as revolutionary movements arising from conditions of intolerable exploitation; and Michels likewise regarded them as potentially revolutionary forces but stressed organizational and psychological forces that tend to undermine their effectiveness. Similarly, not one of the authors analyzed failed to emphasize authority relations as an important variable in their respective schemes, though once again in very different ways—Durkheim as a source of integration, Parsons as crucial ingredients in the processes of social control, Marx as an accessory force in the process of exploitation, and Michels as a force subversive to democracy. My main purpose in this essay, however, has not been to focus on these substantive comparisons and contrasts, but rather to ask what place each variable has in the structure of each theory and what procedures the theorist employs in making it part of his explanations.

The assessment of the scientific strengths and weaknesses of a theory. To summarize, we have asked a number of questions of several diverse theorists in this essay:

What are the central problems that are addressed?

What is the theorist trying to explain?

What are the theorist's basic concepts?

How are the basic concepts identified empirically?

What is the logical structure of the concepts?

How are propositions derived or otherwise generated from the logical structure of the concepts?

How are the propositions made testable?

How are the propositions tested, and what conclusions are drawn?

By asking these questions we have been able to arrive at a number of different comparative assessments of the various theorists. With respect to the specification of an initial problem, Durkheim's theory of suicide appears to possess greater clarity and tidiness than the others, because he selected a relatively identifiable range of data (suicide rates) and asked why groups vary in their suicidal tendencies. Michels' problem—the fate of democracy in organizations—is also relatively simple, but it was clouded by certain ambiguities in the concepts (democracy, organization) he used to pose the problem. Parsons was clear in specifying the range of data that was of concern to him—behavior that was deviant or nonconforming in relation to normative expectations— but posed few specific problems regarding the differential incidence of each kind of deviant behavior. Finally, while Marx concentrated less on specific problems than on producing a massive conceptual system that would generate invariant laws, he did address himself to a wide range of problems connected with the production and distribution of commodities and the relations among the social groups under capitalism. In each case it proved possible to identify more or less precisely the central scientific problem or problems associated with the theory, and to develop particular criticisms of each.

With respect to the issue of logical structure, Michels' formal theory of the origins of oligarchy appears at first glance to be the tightest and most economical but on further analysis proves to be heavily burdened with ambiguities and numerous residual categories that were utilized unsystematically to account for apparent exceptions. Durkheim's structure, involving the paired opposites of egoism-altruism and anomie-fatalism, is also simple in initial formulation, but is likewise fraught with overlapping concepts, vagueness and ambiguities, inconsistent use of variables, and residual categories. Parsons' classification {60} of the directions of deviance is relatively unambiguous, but the relations between this classification and his more general theoretical concepts are unclear, and the relations among the basic explanatory variables—strain, the structuring of deviance, social control, and so on—are incomplete in a variety of ways. Finally, while the structure of Marx's scheme is remarkable for the systematic transition from one basic set of concepts to the next, some of the basic concepts—such as the components of labor, simple average labor, and socially necessary labor—are couched in so many equivocations that the validity of the entire logical structure is thrown into doubt. In each case, the characteristic flaws in logical structure led us to question whether the basic propositions of any of the theories could be considered to be formally derived from the structure of basic concepts.

With respect to the issue of falsifiability, each theory also contained flaws peculiar to itself. Both Durkheim's and Michels' propositions are stated in sufficiently specific empirical form to permit their falsification in principle, but in both cases the authors' tendency to rely on residual categories makes the theories less falsifiable in practice than in principle. Marx developed a theory that generated specific predictions about the future of capitalism, and these clearly are falsifiable; but his theory, too, possesses certain elastic or ambiguous categories, such as class consciousness and exploitation, that can lead to the theory's being correct every time, and therefore unfalsifiable. Finally, Parsons' theory also suffers from a lack of falsifiability, but not so much from the presence of residual categories as from its theoretical incompleteness, which leaves the theory relatively unable to generate specific, testable propositions.

Three cautions in conclusion. By approaching several theories with a common set of questions in mind, we have been able to assess some characteristic scientific strengths and weaknesses of each. Hopefully, however, this exercise should not suggest that any theory can be automatically and completely evaluated by the unimaginative application of this particular checklist of questions. While these questions may have a sensitizing function, their rigid application may blind us to other, perhaps more important points of significance about the theory. Furthermore, the theorist's own purposes should in some sense dictate which critical questions should be asked. If a theorist's objective is mainly classificatory rather than explanatory, questions relating to the logical structure of his categories are clearly more salient than questions relating to the empirical validity of his propositions. Theoretical criticism, in short, should be tailored in part by the objectives and dominant emphases of the theorist himself.

Second, the net assessment of the scientific adequacy of any given theory will seldom turn out to be a simple blanket judgment, but rather a balance of strengths and weaknesses. As the list of criteria indicates, a theory is a multifaceted construction, and many different, independent questions must be asked in assessing it. One type of weakness—for example, an ambiguity in logical structure—does not necessarily mean that the theory will be weak in other respects as well. Moreover, the discovery of even a series of critical weaknesses does not necessarily sound the death knell for an entire theory. One of the central propositions of Marx's *Capital* concerned the positive association between technological improvement and the production of relative surplus value. In examining the structure of Marx's theory, we found that the derivation of the concept of surplus value was marred by a number of equivocations and that the predictions about the future of capitalism based on the association between technology and surplus value were questionable. Marx thus appeared to have erred in arriving at the relationship and, in relying on it, to have generated a number of incorrect predictions. Yet the association may still be a sound one, though for reasons different from the ones adduced by Marx; and if properly combined with other propositions, it may still prove fruitful in explaining and predicting changes in capitalist societies. Finally, the discovery of a scientific weakness may indicate, not that the theory should be discarded, but that it should be supplemented by further refinement. Some shortcomings of Durkheim's theory of suicide appear to call for a more systematic statement of the relations between social and psychological factors. Some of the explanatory incompleteness of Parsons' theory of deviance calls for the further specification of conditions under which strain gives rise to deviance, deviance excites mechanisms of social control, and so on. And some of the questionable uses of residual categories, such as conflict among leaders, in Michels' theory calls for their more formal incorporation into an expanded theory of the dynamics of power and authority.

A final caution concerns the objective of this essay itself. It has not been ventured as a lesson in the art of intellectual destructiveness. It has been written with the conviction that the best means of learning is to test the critical limits of the knowledge to which we are exposed. My objective has been to assist in developing our critical faculties so that they may be more effectively used in confronting the ideas around us, particularly in assessing our own theories about the social world.

INDEX OF SECTIONS

**[Page numbers refer to the pagination of the original edition.
These numbers are inserted into the text within brackets.]**

BIBLIOGRAPHY

Karl Abraham, "A Short Study of the Development of the Libido, Viewed in the Light of Mental Disorders," *Selected Papers on Psychoanalysis.* Hogarth, London, 1924.

Howard S. Becker, *Outsiders: Studies in the Sociology of Deviance.* Free Press, 1963.

Robert N. Bellah, "Durkheim and History." *American Sociological Review,* 1959, 24:447-451.

Eugen von Bohm-Bawerk, *Karl Marx and the Close of His System* (transl. Paul M. Sweezy). Kelley, 1949.

E. H. Carr, *Karl Marx.* Dent, London, 1934.

C. W. Cassenelli, "The Law of Oligarchy." *The American Political Science Review,* 1953, 47:773-784.

Richard A. Cloward, "Illegitimate Means, Anomie, and Deviant Behavior." *American Sociological Review,* 1959, 24:164-176.

Albert K. Cohen, "The Sociology of the Deviant Act: Anomie Theory and Beyond." *American Sociological Review,* 1965, 30:5-14.

Lewis Coser, *The Functions of Social Conflict.* Free Press, 1956.

Ralf Dahrendorf, *Class and Class Conflict in Industrial Society.* Stanford University Press, 1959.

Robert Dubin, "Deviant Behavior and Social Structure." *American Sociological Review,* 1959, 24:147-164.

Èmile Durkheim, *The Division of Labor in Society,* 1897 (transl. George Simpson). Free Press, 1949. Especially Book One, ch. VII.

Èmile Durkheim, *The Rules of the Sociological Method,* 1895 (transl. Sarah A. Solovay and John H. Mueller). Free Press, 1958.

Èmile Durkheim, *Suicide,* 1897 (transl. John A. Spaulding and George Simpson). Free Press, 1951.

Sigmund Freud, "Mourning and Melancholia," *Standard Edition,* vol. 14. Hogarth Press and Institute of Psychoanalysis, London, 1917.

Sigmund Freud, "The Economic Problem of Masochism," *Standard Edition,* vol. 19. Hogarth Press and Institute of Psychoanalysis, London, 1924.

Erving Goffman, *Asylums.* Aldine, 1962.

Andrew Henry and James F. Short, Jr., *Suicide and Homicide.* Free Press, 1954. Especially ch. 2.

Rudolph Hilferding, "Bohm-Bawerk's Criticism of Marx," in Eugen von
    Bohm-Bawerk, *Karl Marx and the Close of His System* (transl. Paul
    M. Sweezy). Kelley, 1949.

Eric Hobsbawn, Introduction to *Pre-Capitalist Economic Formations.*
    International Publishers, 1964.

Barclay D. Johnson, "Durkeim's One Cause of Suicide." *American
    Sociological Review,* 1965, 30:883-886.

Karl Marx, *Capital,* 1867 (transl. Samuel Moore and Edward Aveling).
    George Allen & Unwin, London, 1949.

Karl Marx, *The Communist Manifesto,* 1848. Regnery, 1954.

Karl Marx, *A Contribution to the Critique of Political Economy,* 1859. Kerr,
    1913.

Robert K. Merton, "Conformity, Deviation, and Opportunity-Structures."
    American Sociological Review, 1959, 24:178-189.

Robert K. Merton, *Social Theory and Social Structure.* Free Press, 1968.

Robert Michels, *Political Parties,* 1911 (transl. Eden and Cedar Paul).
    Dover, 1959.

Talcott Parsons, *The Social System.* Free Press, 1951. Especially ch. VII.

Talcott Parsons, *Societies: Evolutionary and Comparative Perspectives.*
    Prentice-Hall, 1966.

Talcott Parsons, *The Structure of Social Action.* McGraw-Hill, 1937.

Talcott Parsons and Edward Shils, eds., *Toward a General Theory of
    Action.* Harvard University Press, 1951.

Whitney Pope, *Emile Durkheim's Theory of Social Integration.*
    Unpublished Ph.D. dissertation, University of California, Berkeley,
    1970.

Hanan C. Selvin, "Durkheim's *Suicide* and Problems of Empirical
    Research." *American Journal of Sociology,* 1958, 63:607-619.

Neil J. Smelser, *Essays in Sociological Explanation.* Prentice-Hall, 1968.
    Especially pp. 58-59.

Neil J. Smelser, *Social Change in the Industrial Revolution.* University of
    Chicago Press, 1959.

Irving Zeitlin, *Ideology and the Development of Sociological Theory.*
    Prentice-Hall, 1968. Especially ch. 15.

About the Author

Neil J. Smelser gained undergraduate degrees from Harvard (Social Relations, 1952) and Oxford (Philosophy, Politics and Economics, 1954), and his Ph.D. from Harvard in 1958. Most of his academic career has been spent in Sociology at the University of California, Berkeley, where he was advanced to the rank of University Professor of Sociology in 1972. Between 1994 and 2001 he was director of the Center for Advanced Study in the Behavioral Sciences (Stanford). His major works include *Economy and Society* (with Talcott Parsons, 1956*), Social Change in the Industrial Revolution* (1959), *Theory of Collective Behavior* (1962; rpt'd Quid Pro, 2011), *Comparative Methods in the Social Sciences* (1976), *Social Paralysis and Social Change* (1991), *The Social Edges of Psychoanalysis* (1998), *The Faces of Terrorism* (2007), and *The Odyssey Experience* (2009). In 2001 he co-edited, with Paul B. Baltes, the 26-volume *International Encyclopedia of the Social and Behavioral Sciences.*

Dr. Smelser has been recognized by election into the American Academy of Arts and Sciences, the American Philosophical Association, and the National Academy of Sciences. In 1996-97 he served as President of the American Sociological Association, and in 2002 he received the first Mattei Dogan Award for a distinguished career in sociology, from the International Sociological Association.

www.quidprobooks.com